D0493153

the big book of
handmade
cards
and gift-wrap

the big book of
handmade
cards
and gift-wrap

over 50 step-by-step projects

vivienne bolton

TED SMART

Dedication
For Michael, Zolii, Bianca, Sophie, Chloe, Ben and Joshua.

This edition produced for
The Book People Ltd
Hall Wood Avenue
Haydock
St Helens WA11 9UL

Published in 2004 by
New Holland Publishers (UK) Ltd
London · Cape Town · Sydney · Auckland

Garfield House
86 – 88 Edgware Road
London W2 2EA
United Kingdom
www.newhollandpublishers.com

80 McKenzie Street
Cape Town 8001
South Africa

14 Aquatic Drive
Frenchs Forest, NSW 2086
Australia

218 Lake Road
Northcote, Auckland
New Zealand

ISBN 1 84330 829 0

Senior Editor: Clare Hubbard
Photographer: Shona Wood
Design: Peter Crump
Template Illustrations: Stephen Dew
Production: Hazel Kirkman
Editorial Direction: Rosemary Wilkinson

5 7 9 10 8 6 4

Reproduction by Modern Age Repro House Ltd, Hong Kong
Printed and bound by Times Offset (M) Sdn. Bhd., Malaysia

Note
The author and publishers have made every effort to ensure that all
instructions given in this book are safe and accurate, but they cannot accept
liability for any resulting injury or loss or damage to either property or
person, whether direct or consequential and howsoever arising.

Acknowledgements
Special thanks to my editor, Clare Hubbard, who is always calm, supportive
and organized. Thanks also to Shona Wood, whose photography complements my work so well,
Rosemary Wilkinson and Corin and Chloe for dreaming up names for the cards.
Thanks also to Fiskars UK Ltd (Newlands Avenue, Bridgend CF31 2XA) for supplying equipment for use in this book.

contents

introduction

I have a clear memory of sitting at a news-paper-covered table in my grandmother's sewing room surrounded by scissors, sticky tape, shiny sweet wrappers and a pad of deckle-edged writing paper. I was squeezing runny, brown glue through an orange rubber lid with a slit in it on to a silver doily. I can't have been more than six or seven years old when I proudly presented that birthday card to my grandfather. I haven't changed much since. I still love paper – be it gift-wrap, brightly decorated foil sweet wrappers, handmade paper or a child's rainbow-coloured writing pad. My range of adhesives has certainly improved, however. I am now the proud owner of a wide variety of tools and craft materials and I've tried just about every craft there is, but inside I am still that little girl getting high on creativity.

I have thoroughly enjoyed designing the cards and gift-wrap for this book. So many different things – colours, textures, materials, memories of places, friends and family – have inspired the designs. Some of the cards were originally made with specific friends or family members in mind: for example, Memories (see page 46) was made as a Mother's Day card for my mother and Magic Number (see page 106) was inspired by the theme we thought up for my youngest grandson's birthday party.

I have particularly enjoyed coordinating gift-wrap and greetings cards. It has given me the opportunity to make good use of stamps and stencils. There's something extremely satisfying about a group of cards, tags, bags, pouches and boxes that all match. It's also an interesting way of developing your design skills.

I am fortunate in having an amazingly well-stocked craft shop just a short drive from my home, along with a variety of art material shops, department stores and cake-decorating shops (yes, you read that correctly, they are a great source of material for the card-maker) in my local town. Experience has taught me to always keep my eyes open when searching for inspiration, new materials and information.

I store anything that I think might be useful one day and with card-making as a hobby I have the perfect excuse to save almost everything. In fact, my stock of craft materials is only controlled by the storage space that I have. Get in to the habit of looking at everything as a potential material for use on a card; you'll surprise yourself with the ideas that you come up with.

Be inspired by the designs in this book and use them as a springboard from which to create your own designs. I hope you get as much pleasure from using this book as I have from designing and making the projects.

Best wishes

Vivienne Bolton

getting started

When starting any new hobby, equipping yourself with the basic tools and materials is part of the fun and this is particularly the case with card-making as there are so many wonderful things now available for the card-maker to buy. Start small with good quality cutting equipment, a selection of paper and card and adhesive tape and glue. As you work your way through the projects in this book you will find that your collection of tools and materials will grow and that your scrap box of bits and pieces will be bursting with all of those interesting things that you've found.

Search out good suppliers, both local stores and mail order companies (a reliable mail-order supplier is invaluable). As well as checking out craft suppliers, look in cake decorating shops and art material outlets. Small stores are often better as they have time for customers and often specialize in certain areas.

If you are fortunate enough to have the space, create a permanent work surface for yourself and devote a cupboard or shelf to the storage of your materials. If space is an issue in your house, make yourself a portable "craft workshop" – a couple of box files to hold materials and equipment, along with a protective surface cover and a large cutting mat. Decorate and label your storage boxes and keep things filed for easy access. I can't emphasize enough how important it is to keep your tools and materials in good order and condition. No matter how much time you spend making a card, it won't look good if the paper is creased or marked or your craft knife is blunt.

The Getting Started section looks at all of the materials and equipment that you will need to complete the projects in this book. Also demonstrated are the basic techniques of scoring, folding and tracing templates. There are sections on card design, decorating envelopes and making gift-wrap.

paper and card

A wide range of paper and card is available in good stationery and craft stores, and through mail-order suppliers (see pages 158–59). Paper and card comes in standard sizes graded from A5 to A1 (A4 is the standard size for most letterhead paper). Although I occasionally purchase paper in larger sheets, I find that A5 (148 x 210mm / 5^{13}/$_{16}$ x 8$\frac{1}{4}$in) and A4 (210 x 297mm / 8$\frac{1}{4}$ x 11^{11}/$_{16}$in) sheets are easiest to handle and are less likely to be damaged in transit or storage. Paper and card cut to A4 size is the most widely available commercially.

From the finest tissue to the thickest card, paper and card are available in almost any shade, weight, quality and texture. I always have a selection of textured and plain white and cream card in stock as many designs seem to begin with a white or cream card base. I also often prepare coloured A5 card bases and store them in a special basket filed by colour.

Consider the texture and thickness of cardboard when choosing sheets for particular projects. While you will need good quality card for a base, paper or thin card is suitable for framing a central feature or for creating layers. I purchase sheets of gift-wrap whenever I see something that inspires me and I save used Christmas and birthday wrapping; you never know when something will be useful. Gift-wrap can be used as a card base but you will need to back it first to give it some stability.

Paper and card are the key raw materials of card-making so you will need a good storage system. Store paper flat and divide it by size, colour and quality so that it is easy to find when you're working. If paper becomes creased you can try smoothing it with a warm iron to restore it to near-perfect condition. Never throw scraps of paper and card away – keep a small box of off-cuts as they will be useful for small projects, collages and layering.

Sugar paper

This thick, slightly textured paper comes in muted shades and is one of the cheapest papers available. Sugar paper is best used as a feature rather than a card base.

Corrugated card and paper

This comes in a variety of corrugations and colours. Use it as a card base or in layering. It is also great for making your own cut-outs and motifs, and is effective wrapping for cylindrical-shaped objects.

Handmade paper

It is available in soft, pastel colours, through to rich, jewel-like shades. The prettiest papers often have flower petals and leaves embedded in them, giving the papers a wonderful texture. Handmade paper comes in a variety of weights and the thicker papers can be used to create the card blank. Used in layering or to create backgrounds handmade paper always creates an interesting feature. See pages 148–49 for a gallery of gift-wrap made using handmade papers.

Mulberry paper

This is a light, opaque paper that is handmade from mulberry leaves and contains strands of silk. It is available in many colours, is lightweight and has a slight textured pattern which can be very effective when used creatively. Mulberry paper can be attached with aerosol glue.

Metallic paper

These papers are good highlighters and are effective when used to create borders, frames and cut-outs. They come in a variety of finishes – some muted others glossy. Metallic paper is easily damaged so should be stored properly. It is advisable to put layers of tissue paper between each sheet.

Translucent paper

I love the softness and depth you can create with these papers. When layered on other colours or white they bring a special

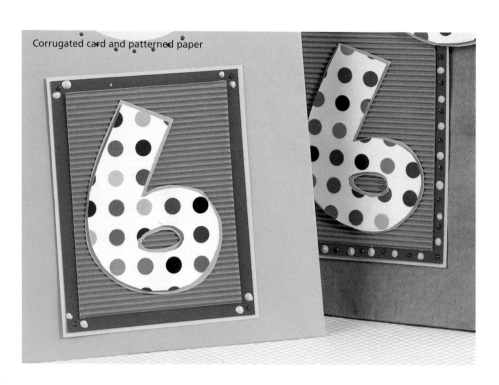
Corrugated card and patterned paper

quality to cards. Translucent paper can be used as a card base but it should be backed with card to give it some substance.

Vellum

This is a semi-opaque paper available plain or patterned. It is very useful for layering.

Plasma

Plasma is a versatile heavyweight, translucent plastic. It is very flexible so is useful for pop-ups. Attach with double-sided tape or glue dots.

Patterned paper

Commercially available patterned paper and gift-wrap can be the basis of wonderful cards. They are useful for backgrounds or to cut motifs from. Make bags and cover gift-boxes with gift-wrap to create coordinated gift sets. Store gift-wrap rolled or flat.

Table napkins and paper hankies

These are a delightful decorative material source. I have found paper hankies printed with frogs, umbrellas and roses and table napkins are available in a wide variety of designs. Use aerosol glue to attach these

materials to cards and don't forget to separate the patterned layer first.

Angel hair paper

A stiff, gauzy paper/fabric useful for layers..

Angel hair

The notes on pages 9–15 are general information on the variety of products and materials that are available to the card-maker. You should always follow the manufacturer's instructions for the specific products that you buy.

pens, pencils and paints

Pens

I always have a good handwriting pen and a black and blue fine liner to hand. Fine liners are very useful and come in a wide range of colours.

Pencils

Pencils are graded by the hardness of the lead. HB is the all-purpose pencil – the lead is neither hard nor soft. If you want a fine line choose an H or HH; if you need a soft, dark line then go for a 3B or 4B. I always keep a selection of pencils. My favourite pencil is a propelling one that contains a soft lead. It is easy to erase when marking up and is lovely to write with and to draw out rough designs.

Marker pens

Useful for creating designs on plasma or vellum. A double-ended fine/broad point pen in black is my favourite. I use a marker pen when transferring patterns as the marks are clear, clean and easy to see.

Silver and gold pens

I find fine nib silver and gold pens very useful when writing on cards, particularly on black paper or card. Liquid silver and gold pens are also useful but test them out on your paper first as the ink sometimes bleeds. It is important to replace the lid immediately after use.

Gel pens

These highly versatile pens are lovely to decorate cards with. The quality of the ink is very good and the colours are amazing. You can write with one gel pen over another and they are effective on light and dark papers.

Felt-tip pens

Felt-tip pens are always useful as they come in such a variety of thicknesses and colours, and are an economical option. They are good for marking up edgings and try creating rainbow borders with different shades. Use them for highlighting, writing messages inside cards and to ink up intricate rubber stamp designs in place of an inkpad.

3D Paint

3D paint can be used as a paint or a glue. Use it to decorate, embellish or stick. Great for highlighting, patterns and corner features. 3D paint comes in a rainbow of colours. A gem effect can be created using coloured, translucent 3D paints.

Pencil

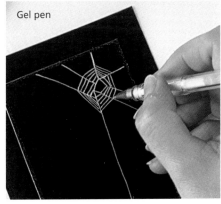

Gel pen

3D paint

cutting and scoring equipment

Scissors

Make sure you have small and large paper scissors, fine-tipped scissors for cut-outs and other intricate work and scissors with a patterned edge. Keep a pair of scissors specifically for cutting fabric. My Fiskars non-stick scissors are one of my most useful tools. I use them for cutting glued surfaces and sticky tape.

Craft knife

A sharp craft knife is essential for cutting neat edges. Great care should be taken when using them – always use a metal ruler, work on a cutting mat and don't cut towards your body. Replace the safety lid

after use and keep the knife in a safe place well out of the reach of children.

Cutting mat

Invest in a cutting mat marked with clear measure lines.

Stylus

Use a stylus to ensure a neat fold line is scored on paper and card.

Rulers and measuring

Buy a metal ruler for cutting against and a clear plastic ruler for taking measurements. A set square is essential for drawing accurate right angles.

Shape cutters and templates

I find shape cutting tools and templates extremely useful and often wonder what I did without them. They make cutting out shaped windows and frames so much easier. Once you have mastered the technique of using the tools, squares, circles, ovals and rectangles are quick and easy to cut. Always cut on a board or a mat. Practise on scrap paper and card in order to produce good finished pieces. I have used these tools throughout the book, but don't worry if you don't have them; you can just cut the ovals, squares etc. using scissors or a craft knife. I have included templates where appropriate.

adhesives

Keep a selection of adhesives at hand. Always replace lids and store them correctly.

PVA glue

This glue becomes transparent when dry and is useful for sticking paper to card or card to card. I transfer a quantity of PVA glue to a small squeezy applicator for ease of use. I find this incredibly useful when small quantities of glue are necessary and the narrow applicator tube is easy to keep clear and covered.

Glue stick

A glue stick is a useful alternative to PVA glue or adhesive tape. Keep the glue stick clean and always replace the lid to prevent the glue drying out.

Aerosol glue

Useful when sticking tissue paper, mulberry paper, fabric or opaque paper. When using this type of adhesive I always use what I call a "glue box". This is a cardboard carton approximately 40cm (16in) square. Place the item to be sprayed in the base of the box. Spray with adhesive then close the lid of the box to minimize the inhalation of fumes and glue particles. Remove the sprayed item after a few minutes. Always follow the manufacturer's instructions for the specific type of glue that you buy.

Glue marker pen

Perfect for attaching decorative motifs and other small items. When a little sparkle is required draw lines/patterns or write text with the glue marker pen and then sprinkle glitter over the glue. For a raised finish sprinkle with embossing powder and fix with a precision heat tool (see page 14).

Glitter glue

Useful as an embellishment. Can be used to attach acetate decoratively.

Adhesive tape

This comes in a selection of widths. A good, clear, low-tack tape is very useful.

Double-sided tape

Double sided tape is wonderful. I love it. You will see how much I love it by how many times I've used it in the projects in this book! Quick and easy to use, double-sided tape comes in a variety of widths and is also available in dispensers which save you cutting little pieces. Use double-sided tape instead of glue for a clean finish.

3D tape

This is a double-sided tape with an added spongy layer enabling you to create raised pictures or embellishments.

Glue dots

Excellent when a 3D effect is required. Good for attaching buttons etc. Be careful, as they are very sticky!

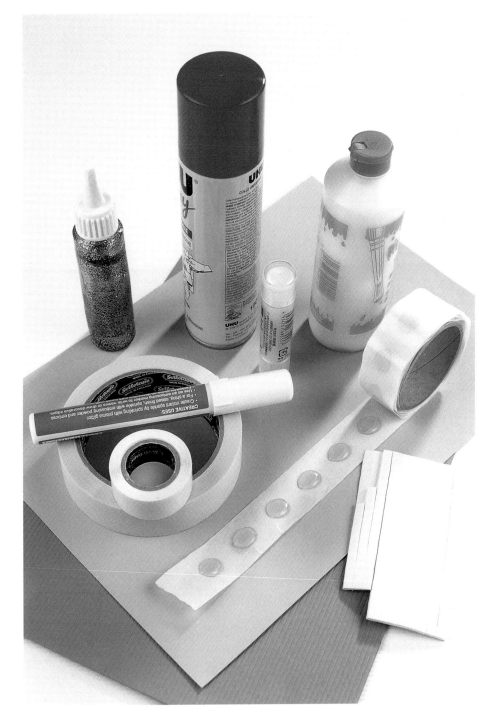

stamps and punches

Stamps

Stamps are available in a huge variety of styles and designs; some even have messages on them. Some are extremely versatile, others you may use only once. Use stamps to create your own motifs and borders. Keep your stamps clean; wash in warm soapy water or use stamp cleaner. See pages 144–45 for a gallery of gift-wrap made using rubber stamps.

Coloured ink pads

Use coloured ink pads or felt-tip pens to colour rubber stamps.

Embossing pads

These can be clear or coloured. You simply stamp your design on to the card and sprinkle it with embossing powder.

Embossing pen

Use an embossing pen along with embossing powder for freehand embossing. Do not use regular felt-tip pens as their ink dries too quickly.

Embossing powders

Embossing powders used with stamps are such fun. Always sprinkle embossing powder over a sheet of scrap paper, shake and return any surplus powder to the container for reuse.

Precision heat tool

A heat tool is necessary to fix embossing powder. These tools get extremely hot so do take care. Keep your hands and the paper or card that is being heated a safe distance from the heat source (try holding the paper with tweezers or tongs). Take care not to singe the paper. Always follow the manufacturer's instructions.

Homemade stamps

Cut out simple designs from a foam sheet and use double-sided tape to attach them to a piece of card or sponge board. Use as you would a commercial stamp. The holly printed gift-wrap on page 119 was made using a homemade stamp.

Punches

Punches are such fun. You can punch out patterns and motifs. Use the punched out shapes to create your own motifs and to decorate cards, boxes, bags and wrapping paper. A simple hole punch can be a useful tool too.

decorative materials

Rivets and eyelets

These are great to use in card designs. You usually buy the rivets and eyelets in a kit along with a hole maker and a tool to hammer the reverse of the eyelets flat. These are obtainable from craft and dress-making shops. You will need a hammer and a sturdy board to work on. I use a wooden breadboard and a lightweight hammer.

Wire

This comes in a variety of colours and thicknesses. Some outlets stock little peg boards which can be used for shaping wire. To cut wire you will need a small pair of pliers or a pair of scissors kept specifically for this purpose.

Buttons and beads

An interesting bead or button can be the focus of a special card. I purchase them in junk shops, cut them off old clothes and seek them out in haberdashery stores.

Braid, ribbon and mesh

Ribbons, strings, threads and yarns are useful for making handles on gift-bags and as extra decoration on a card.

Gems

Faux gems add a little luxury to your cards. Use tiny gems as accents. Try haberdashery departments for a selection of unusual stick-on gems.

Glitter

Glitter or sparkle is useful when embellishing cards or making motifs. I prefer the finer glitters and occasionally use glittery embossing powder as glitter.

Oven-bake clay

Using this material is your chance to craft something unique. Useful for making small hearts, flowers, stars etc. Follow the manufacturer's instructions.

Transfers

There are a huge variety of designs available in many different styles – beautiful illustrations, comic characters, patterns etc. Transfers are an extemely quick way to make an original card. Peel-offs are widely available and can be used on acetate or vellum and decorated with felt-tips to create stained glass effects.

Motifs, cut-outs and stickers

There is such a wide variety of motifs and cut-outs available, you are bound to find something to suit your needs. Some are adhesive, others you will need to glue on. Look in haberdashery departments, cake decorating stores and stationery and craft shops. See pages 142–43 for a gallery of gift-wrap made using stickers and motifs.

card design

Crafters are always on the lookout for new ideas. I keep a journal where I note down and sketch out ideas for all sorts of things from greetings card designs to ideas for fundraiser sales, wedding cake designs, sketches of baby knits or ideas for new recipes. Very often, something that I had intended for one project, works for another. I tape in bits and pieces torn from magazines and inspirational photos taken on holiday. When I have a new project to create a design for, the first place I go to for inspiration is my journal. It is amazing how the roughest of sketches will remind me of a jumper I saw someone wearing when I was travelling on the Paris Metro or a beach bag I noticed on a trip to the seaside. Simply make a record of anything that catches your "design" eye, as you never know when you might be able to use it.

I also have a large noticeboard where I pin up an on-going collection of inspirational pictures and tear-outs. I position it so that I can see it from where I'm working, so my brain is always thinking of new ideas. When the noticeboard becomes overcrowded I tape the most useful images into some sort of order in my journal.

I file bits and pieces of paper and card left over from design projects in themes and colourways. For example, scraps of Christmas gift-wrap, brightly coloured sweet wrappers, the foil from Christmas crackers, Christmas stickers, used Christmas postage stamps torn from envelopes and Christmas cards to be cut up and recycled get put in a box file and labelled "Christmas". When the festive season is approaching I sit down and go through the box searching for inspiration. I also keep themed boxes for spring, flowers, new baby and things suitable for childrens' cards. Having everything in one place is very useful, particularly when making homemade motifs.

Homemade motifs

I find commercially available motifs very useful and would not be without them.

However, occasionally when I have the time, I make my own motifs. I find this very creative as it gives me a chance to play with my materials when I am not under pressure to produce a card for a particular person or client. I save scraps left over from other projects and store them in a large box; my "motif" box. I keep punched out shapes, interesting scraps of paper and card, stickers, ribbons, buttons – basically I don't throw anything away.

A few ideas as to the kinds of motifs that you can make are shown in the photograph below. Take the black cat motif for example. One is made from a stamped image decorated with green gel pen eyes. The image is layered up on paper and card which outline and frame the picture. The other is a silver embossed cat, layered on to different coloured cards. You can use the same stamp, punch, sticker or paper to create many different motifs. Change the colour of the ink, card, paper or pen or cut the backing layers into different shapes and sizes.

scoring and folding

Scoring makes folding card and paper easy and gives your finished cards a professional appearance.

Use a stylus to score paper and card. You should score on the outside of the card.

Hill and valley folds are basic origami folds and are useful to the card-maker. I have used them in the Winter Wonderland card on pages 124-125.

A hill fold is scored on the front of the card and folded so that the fold peaks towards you.

A valley fold is scored on the underside of the card so that the fold points away from you.

Hill fold

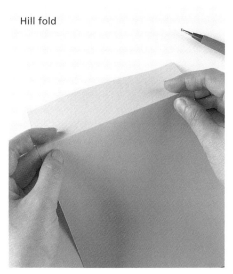

Scoring

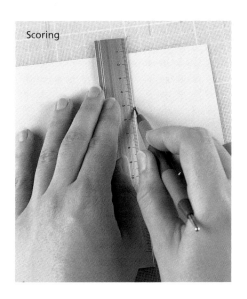

Valley fold

tracing templates

There are several ways of doing this, and you may already have your own way that you're happy with, so carry on! I like to trace templates and patterns on to acetate using a marker pen, especially when I'm making templates for envelope inserts, gift pouches, bags – indeed any pattern that I intend using more than once. Obviously you can using tracing paper, but acetate is more robust and your templates will stay in good condition for longer.

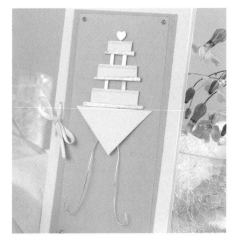

decorating envelopes

I'm not going to show you how to make envelopes as they are available to buy in just about every size and colour imaginable. I think it is more efficient to spend your time decorating envelopes to match your cards. Use stickers or motifs to decorate envelope covers. It is also fun to create inserts. You can use decorative paper, or line the envelope with tissue or mulberry paper and then use punches, stamps, gel pens, whatever you can think of, to embellish the lining. Have fun and let your imagination run away with you.

1 Select an envelope that you want to decorate and use it to create a template for the lining. Do this with acetate and a marker pen.

2 Use the template to cut out an insert from your chosen paper.

3 Use aerosol glue (or double-sided tape) to attach the insert inside the envelope.

1

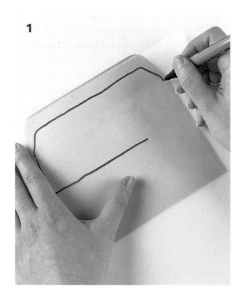

2

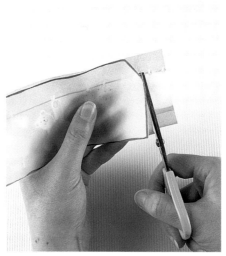

3

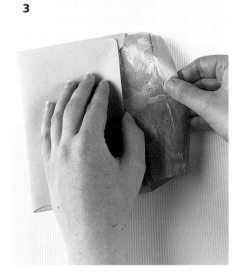

gift-wrap

Making gift-wrap to coordinate with your cards is another way to use your design skills. It's your chance to create gorgeous wrapping papers, boxes, bags and pouches that are much more desirable than anything you'll find in the shops. Obviously you need to think about how you can take the design elements on the card and carry them through. I often use the feature stencil, stamp or theme of the card. For example with Flower Power (pages 58–9) simply sticking the punched flowers on paper looked good; while for Holly Berries (pages 122–3) I made my own stamp. The foil decorated card Star Bright (pages 126–7) looks great paired with embossed gold snowflake stamped tissue paper.

Take care to ensure that the shades of paper or card you use are the same as those on your card, or complement the card. Also, remember to use the same embossing powders, paints and pens. It is this attention to detail that will give your work a professional look.

See pages 142–49 for lots more gift-wrap ideas.

Creating decorative gift-wrap

The ways in which you can decorate gift-wrap are virtually limitless. Paper can be stamped, embossed, stencilled, decorated with punched shapes, covered in stickers – the list goes on and on. Look carefully at the card that you have made and decide how you can use part of the design on your gift-wrap and choose what paper to use as a base.

Tissue paper is my favourite wrapping medium as it is a great background for all sorts of embellishment. It is widely available in a huge range of colours and shades so you'll always find something suitable. I usually use two layers of tissue paper to wrap a gift – one is decorated and the other, plain backing. Use single sheets of decorated tissue to pack out boxes containing delicate or smaller gifts such as lingerie, baby clothes or jewellery.

Brown paper printed or stencilled with gold or silver seasonal motifs makes great Christmas wrapping. White butcher's paper or lining paper looks great printed in primary colours – children's handprints or paint splatters look particularly effective.

Pouches, bags and boxes

Decorating commercially available gift-bags, boxes and pouches is quick and fun. They are available in all shapes, sizes and colours and you can add your own personal touches to them in a matter of minutes. Although it is nice to make your own bags and boxes, buying blanks is certainly the easiest option if you need to decorate 30 party bags or 100 wedding favours. However, even very plain gift-bags can be expensive so look out for other bags that you could use. Plain brown and white paper bags are cheap to buy and make great party bags; recycle gift-bags and boxes that are given to you. Everything that you buy these days seems to come with loads of packaging, so think about how you can reuse it.

If you need a bag of a particular size you may need to make one yourself (see page 21 for instructions). If you need a large bag make it from heavier paper. If this isn't possible, line the paper before you begin construction.

gift pouch

This simple gift pouch is easy to make and fun to decorate. Make pouches in different colours and decorate them to coordinate with your card or gift-wrap.

you will need
A5 sheet acetate
Marker pen
Craft knife
Cutting mat
A5 sheet medium-weight card
Low-tack masking tape
Scissors
Pencil
Stylus
Metal ruler
Eraser
Double-sided tape

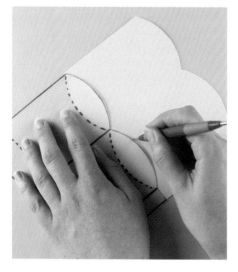

1 Trace the template on page 150 on to acetate using the marker pen. Cut out the template. Lay the template on to the sheet of card and tack in position using low-tack masking tape. Draw around the template in pencil.

2 Use the stylus (and ruler when appropriate) to score the fold lines. Erase any visible pencil lines carefully before folding the scored lines.

3 Place a line of double-sided tape on the flap, fold over and stick. Your pouch is now ready to decorate.

gift-bag

Making a gift-bag is simple. Use plain or patterned paper and make handles from string, rolled paper or ribbon. The main thing to remember when making a gift-bag is that the side folds should be the same depth as the bottom fold. Once you have mastered the technique making bags will be quick and easy. Choose the size of your piece of paper to suit the gift that you want to put in the bag. You can punch holes in the top of the bag and thread ribbon through it or attach bought or homemade handles using PVA glue.

you will need
Sheet of paper
Double-sided tape
Scissors

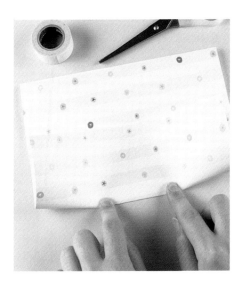

1 Take the side of the paper furthest away from you and fold it down towards the centre. Then fold the side of the paper nearest to you up towards the centre. Make sure that the ends overlap slightly. Use double-sided tape to stick down.

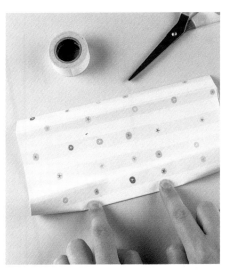

2 Fold the far side in 2cm (¾in). Press down on the fold firmly. Fold the near side in 2cm (¾in) and once again press down on the fold firmly.

3 Open out and push the folds that you have just made, inwards.

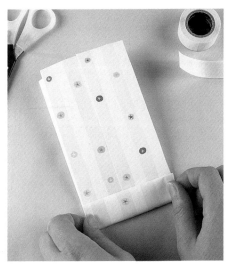

4 Place the folded bag on the surface in front of you. Fold the base of the bag up by 2cm (¾in). Press along the fold firmly. Make a second 2cm (¾in) fold upwards and stick in place with double-sided tape.

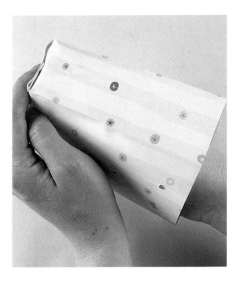

5 Open up the bag by slipping your hand inside it and gently pressing out the corners.

general greetings

projects

ship ahoy

This card has a jaunty seaside theme and is decorated with rub-on transfers. Transfers are a quick and easy way to decorate gift pouches and gift-bags as well.

you will need

- A5 sheet white linen finish card
- Stylus
- Metal ruler
- Blue card
- Silver card
- Blue glitter paper
- Craft knife
- Cutting mat
- Pencil
- Double-sided tape
- Scissors
- Rub-on transfer
- Transfer stick

timing Once the card layers are cut to size this card takes no time at all to make.

alternative Use a flower transfer on a white background, layer it on to coordinating paper and attach to a pastel card base to create a Mother's Day card.

1 Score and fold the sheet of white card to create the card base. To create the layers cut a 5.5cm (2¼in) square from blue card; a 5cm (2in) square from silver card; and a 4.5cm (1¾in) square from blue glitter paper. Use double-sided tape to attach the squares in an upper central position on the card.

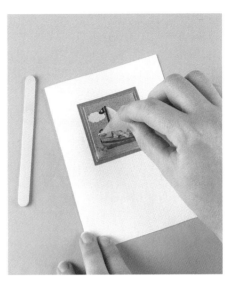

2 Cut around the transfer you wish to use, leaving a 5mm (¼in) border. Remove the backing sheet. Place the transfer on the blue glitter paper and use the transfer stick to rub over the image. Gently peel off the plastic sheet.

There are literally hundreds of different transfer designs available.

3 Cut out the accent decorations and transfer first the sun, then the cloud to the top right-hand corner. Transfer the fish on the left beneath the motif.

4 Finally place a small transfer on the back of the card. This added extra gives your card a professional finish.

friendly frogs

Cheeky frog stickers and 3D paint on brightly decorated card create a great child's birthday card or simply a cheering message to a friend.

you will need

- A5 sheet navy blue card
- Metal ruler
- Stylus
- A5 sheet yellow translucent paper
- Craft knife
- Cutting mat
- Pencil
- Aerosol glue
- A4 sheet white card
- Double-sided tape
- Scissors
- Blue card
- Yellow card
- Black card
- Green card
- 3D adhesive tape
- Suitable frog stickers
- Green and blue 3D paint

timing Take your time when measuring and cutting the layers as they are the focus of the card.

alternative A row of robins on red, white and brown card layers would create a fun, seasonal card. For other animal-theme cards try three sheep with shades of pastel green, white and pink, or pink pigs on brown, white and cream.

1 Score and fold the sheet of dark blue card to create the card blank. Cut a 12.5 x 9cm (5 x 3½in) rectangle of yellow translucent paper. Spray it with aerosol glue and stick it to a piece of white card to back it. Cut away the excess white card.

2 Attach the backed yellow paper centrally to the front of the card blank with double-sided tape.

3 Cut a rectangle of blue card 7.5 x 4cm (3 x 1½in) and use double-sided tape to place it centrally on the yellow paper. Cut a piece of yellow card 6 x 2.5cm (2½ x 1in) and layer this onto the blue card.

4 Cut a 5.5 x 2cm (2¼ x ¾in) rectangle of white card and tape it to the black card. Cut a narrow frame. Tape the framed white card to a piece of green card and cut away all but a narrow frame.

5 Create a 3D effect on the final layer of your card. Place three pieces of 3D tape on the back of the framed white card and stick it on the central panel on the card.

6 Starting with the frog in the middle, place three stickers on the white card. Frame the motif with spots of blue 3D paint and finally squeeze a green spot of paint in each corner of the blue card. If you have a spare sticker attach it to the reverse of the card.

indigo blue

Turn your snapshots into mini masterpieces. Here, the deep blue decorated paper complements the bark and green ivy in the photograph. For more ideas on ways to use this paper see pages 136–37.

you will need

- A4 sheet white card
- Craft knife
- Metal ruler
- Cutting mat
- Pencil
- Aerosol glue
- Sheet indigo blue decorative paper
- Chosen photograph
- Double-sided tape
- Scissors
- Dark blue card

timing Once you have chosen your image, this card is super quick to make.

alternative You could use any photograph in this way – perhaps shots of holidays or family occasions. For a good result it is important to spend time choosing the paper that will frame your image.

1 Cut the sheet of A4 card in half (to create two A5 pieces. Score and fold one half to create the card base. Spray a layer of aerosol glue on the exterior of the card base. Lay it on the sheet of decorative paper and cut away the excess paper with a craft knife.

2 Draw a 6 x 4cm (2½ x 1½in) rectangle around an area of your chosen photograph and cut it out.

3 Use double-sided tape to attach the photograph to a small piece of dark blue card. Use scissors to cut away all but a 5mm (¼in) frame.

4 Use double-sided tape to attach the framed photograph to a small piece of white card and once again cut away all but a 5mm (¼in) frame. Attach the layered motif in an upper central position on the front of the card.

how does your garden grow?

Flowers and accent beads are used to good effect in this earthy card. This card is a perfect greeting for a friend who spends all of their free time in the garden.

you will need

- A5 sheet of speckled buff card
- Metal ruler
- Stylus
- Rectangle cutter, template and board
- White card
- Scissors
- Pencil
- Green card
- Craft knife
- Cutting mat
- Double-sided tape
- Blue translucent paper
- Aerosol glue
- Sheet scrap paper
- Brown and silver mix accent beads
- Plants, watering can and garden tools cut-outs

timing While away a pleasant half hour making this card for a gardening friend.

alternative Try a snow scene using white accent beads on a blue background decorated with dark cut-out branches and a tiny robin redbreast sticker.

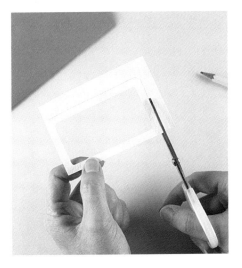

1 Score and fold the sheet of speckled buff card to create the card base. Use the rectangle cutter to cut a 3.75 x 7.5cm (1½ x 3in) rectangular window from white card. Cut a narrow border around the window.

2 Cut out a 4.25 x 8cm (1¾ x 3¼in) rectangle of green card. Use double-sided tape to attach it in an upper central position on the card front. Measure and cut out a piece of blue translucent paper, 4.5 x 4cm (1¾ x 1½in). Use aerosol glue to attach it to the upper half of the green card.

3 Attach a strip of double-sided tape to cover a little of the blue and a little of the green card. Fold a sheet of scrap paper in half and open it out. Put the card on to the scrap paper and sprinkle accent beads over the tape. Do this gently as these little beads roll everywhere! Shake the card to remove any loose beads and return them to the pot.

4 Use double-sided tape to stick the white frame on top of the green and blue rectangle. The garden is now ready for planting with flowers and foliage.

5 Stick the watering can, flowers and tools cut-outs in place. If you are unable to buy prepared cut-outs, make your own from scraps of paper and card using the templates on page 150.

sew simple

Buttons, lace and workbox-themed paper create the perfect card for a crafty friend.

you will need

- A4 sheet blue card
- Craft knife
- Cutting mat
- Metal ruler
- Pencil
- Stylus
- Suitable decorative paper
- Double-sided tape
- Scissors
- A5 sheet white card
- Green translucent paper
- White ricrac
- 3 blue buttons

timing A quick card suitable for birthday greetings or a thank-you note.

alternative Themed paper is easy to find in craft shops. A sheet of romantically decorated paper and a framed row of pretty pearl buttons would make a lovely wedding card.

1 Cut the sheet of blue card in half (to create two A5 pieces). Score and fold one half to make the card base. Cut out an 8.5 x 12.5cm (3½ x 5in) rectangle from the decorated paper. Use double-sided tape to attach it to the white card. Cut away all but a thin frame around the paper. Use double-sided tape to attach the framed picture centrally on the card front.

2 Cut a piece of white card, 2 x 5cm (¾ x 2in). Use double-sided tape to attach this to a piece of blue card. Cut away all but a narrow frame. Next, layer this up on green translucent paper using double-sided tape. Cut a narrow frame around the blue card.

variation *Make up this design in other colourways, using interesting buttons as a central feature.*

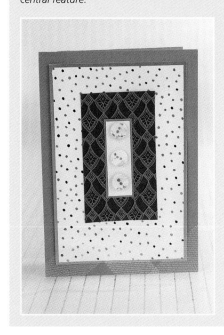

3 Use double-sided tape to attach the layered design to white card. Cut a 5mm (¼in) frame. Place thin strips of double-sided tape around the white frame. Lay the ricrac on the tape to stick it down firmly. Trim. Layer up on to blue card and cut a 5mm (¼in) border.

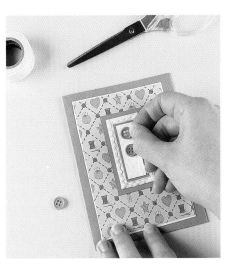

4 Use double-sided tape to attach the framed picture centrally on the card front. Tape the buttons on to the card layers. You might want to add a little decoration to the back of the card. Try using a motif cut from the decorative paper.

pastimes

Hobbies and pastimes make good starting points when designing a card for a friend or relative.

you will need

- A5 sheet olive green card
- Metal ruler
- Pencil
- Craft knife
- Cutting mat
- Stylus
- A5 sheet dark red card
- Double-sided tape
- Scissors
- A5 sheet dark green card
- A5 sheet cream card
- Suitable decorated ribbon
- Small piece black card
- Golf shoes and club (cake decorations)
- Super glue
- Hole punch
- PVA glue
- Small piece white card
- Gold 3D paint
- Flower sticker

 **timing** This card is extremely quick to make.

alternative Both craft and cake decorating stores stock a wide variety of hobby-related decorative items, so you can create many different cards using this design as a base.

1 Cut out a 13.5 x 14cm (5¼ x 5½in) rectangle of olive green card. Score and fold in half to create the card base.

2 Cut out a 10.5 x 5.5cm (4¼ x 2¼in) rectangle of dark red card. Use double-sided tape to attach it in an upper central position on the front of the card.

3 Take the dark green card and cut out a 9.5 x 4.5cm (3¾ x 1¾in) rectangle. Use double-sided tape to attach it centrally on the dark red card. Measure and cut out a 9 x 4cm (3½ x 1½in) rectangle from cream card. Use double-sided tape to stick it on top of the dark green card.

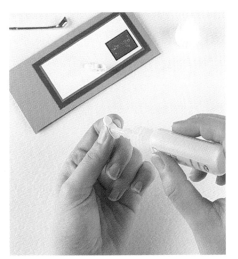

4 Your card is now ready to decorate. Cut a piece of ribbon so that the motif is in the centre and use double-sided tape to attach to a piece of black card. Cut away all but a narrow frame. Tape it in the upper right-hand corner of the cream card. Use super glue to stick the golf shoes and club in place.

5 Punch three small circles out of white card and use PVA glue to stick them in a row beneath the framed picture. Paint a gold 3D dot in the corners of the dark red card. Put the flower sticker in the bottom right-hand corner.

eastern promise

The design for this versatile card was inspired by the ornately decorated wrapping paper. Use the

paper to decorate tags, pouches and boxes.

you will need

- A4 sheet of cream card
- Craft knife
- Pencil
- Metal ruler
- Set square
- Cutting mat
- Stylus
- Embossing stamp pad
- Suitable rubber stamp
- Sheet of scrap paper
- Gold embossing powder
- Tweezers or tongs
- Precision heat tool
- Wrapping paper with Oriental pattern
- Double-sided tape
- Scissors
- Gold paper

1 Cut a 13 x 26cm (5 x 10¼in) rectangle out of the cream card. Make small light pencil marks at 3cm (1in), 8cm (3in), 18cm (7in) and 23cm (9in). These indicate where the folds will be. Using the set square and stylus make hill folds at 3cm (1in) and 23cm (9in), and valley folds at 8cm (3in) and 18cm (7in).

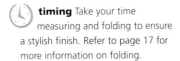

timing Take your time measuring and folding to ensure a stylish finish. Refer to page 17 for more information on folding.

alternative All you need to do to create a totally different card is to choose another stamp and different paper.

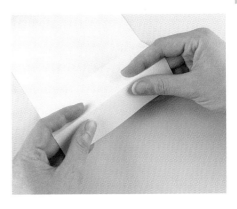

2 Carefully fold the card into shape.

3 Open up the card and, using the embossing stamp pad, stamp the shape in a central position on the open card base. Place the stamped card on to a sheet of scrap paper. Sprinkle with the gold embossing powder. You need to do this before the ink dries.

4 Shake the excess powder on to the scrap paper and return it to the container. Holding the stamped card with tweezers or tongs, heat the powdered design with the precision heat tool until glossy and set.

5 The card is now ready for decoration. Cut two pieces of patterned paper 2.5 x 13cm (1 x 5in). Use double-sided tape to attach the pieces to the open edges of the card. Cut two more pieces of patterned paper, this time 5 x 13cm (2 x 5in), and attach to the reverse fold with double-sided tape.

6 Cut two 10cm (4in) long strips of gold paper. One should be 5mm (¼in) wide and the other 2.5mm (⅛in) wide. Attach them one above the other, approximately 2cm (¾in) from the bottom of the card.

peacock feather

Clean whites and shimmer gold give this card an air of sophisticated understatement. Use this card as a party or wedding invitation, to say thank-you or send birthday greetings. This versatile stamp can be used in so many colourways, see pages 138–39 for inspiration.

you will need

- A5 sheet cream textured card
- Stylus
- Metal ruler
- Craft knife
- Cutting mat
- Pencil
- Embossing pad
- Peacock feather stamp
- Sheet plain white card
- Scrap paper
- Gold embossing powder
- Precision heat tool
- Double-sided tape
- Scissors
- Sheet shimmer gold card
- Sheet white parchment
- Gold 3D paint

 **timing** Stamped cards are quick and easy to make therefore suitable for mass-production.

alternative Use a poppy stamp and emboss it in brilliant red and green to create a different, but still very stylish, card.

Create a decorative frame using a corner cutter and mount a wonderfully coloured feather in it.

1 Trim the cream textured card to 19cm (7½in) wide. Score and fold to create the card base. Using the embossing stamp pad, print a single peacock feather on a sheet of plain white card.

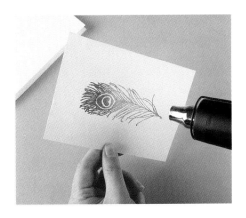

3 Use the precision heat tool to set the embossed design.

5 Use double-sided tape to attach the design to a piece of gold card. Cut away all but a narrow frame.

2 Fold a sheet of scrap paper in half. Hold the stamped white card over the paper and sprinkle with gold embossing powder. Shake off the excess powder and return it to the container.

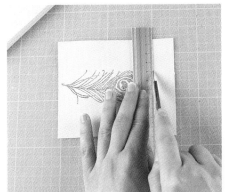

4 Once the paper has cooled, measure a 10.5 x 5cm (4 x 2in) rectangle around the embossed design so that it is in the centre. Cut out.

6 Attach the framed design to a sheet of parchment. Cut away all but a 1cm (½in) frame. Attach with double-sided tape to the card front and decorate with four gold 3D paint dots; one in each corner of the parchment frame.

bead dolly

Plastic beads and bead boards have been a part of my life for as many years as I have

had children. They can be used to create both simple and intricate designs.

you will need

- A5 sheet of plasma
- Stylus
- Metal ruler
- A5 sheet white paper
- Double-sided tape
- Scissors
- Paper napkin with suitable design
- Aerosol glue
- Red, flesh, blue and yellow heat seal beads and board

timing Bead art takes time and patience, have fun creating your own designs.

alternative A bead Christmas decoration would look good on a plasma base with a seasonal edging cut from a Christmas napkin. Make the decoration removable so that it can be used on the tree for years to come.

1 Score and fold the plasma in half. Score and fold the white paper in half and attach it inside the plasma using double-sided tape.

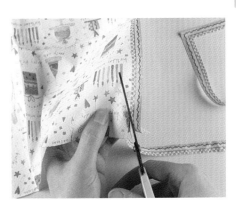

2 Cut out the border pattern from the paper napkin. Separate the patterned layer from the backing layers.

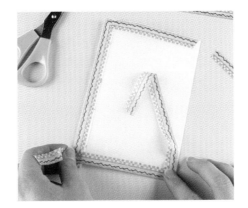

3 Use aerosol glue to attach the border around the edge of the plasma cover. Cut away any excess and be sure to mitre the corners.

4 Use the pattern on page 150 to make up the dolly design using beads and the bead board. Heat seal the beads following the manufacturer's instructions. Use double-sided tape to attach the bead dolly centrally on the card.

variations *These cards were created by my children. Use beads to create simple designs, geometric patterns and pictures. You can make a card suitable for any occasion.*

olive branch

The dove of peace flies across a glittering sky holding an olive branch. For an alternative design create a sunny, rainbow-filled sky.

you will need

- Oval cutter, template and board
- A5 sheet blue card
- Scrap paper
- Aerosol glue
- Spangle glitter
- A5 sheet olive green card
- A5 sheet white textured card

- Double-sided tape
- Scissors
- Acetate
- Fine point black pen
- White card scrap
- Spring green card scrap
- PVA glue

timing This card takes a little time as you need to take care when cutting out the various elements.

alternative A red card base and gold oval could frame a winter backdrop featuring a chubby snowman with a carrot nose.

1 Use the oval cutter, template and board to cut out a 10 x 7.5cm (4 x 3in) oval in blue card. If you do not have an oval cutter use the template on page 151.

2 Fold a sheet of scrap paper in half and open it out. Coat the blue oval with aerosol glue and, holding it over the scrap paper, sprinkle it with spangle glitter. Shake off the excess glitter and return it to the container.

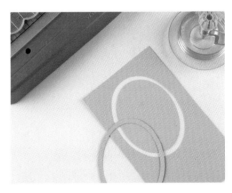

3 Using the oval cutter cut a 10 x 7.5cm (4 x 3in) oval from olive green card. Now cut a second, slightly smaller oval from the centre of the first. You now have a frame. If you do not have an oval cutter use the template on page 151.

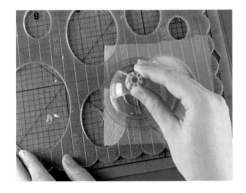

4 Score and fold the sheet of white textured card to create the card blank. Use double-sided tape to attach the blue oval in a central position on the front of the card. Tape the green frame directly on top of the blue oval.

5 Trace the dove and olive branch templates on page 135. Cut the dove pieces out of white card and the olive branch from spring green card. Use PVA glue to attach the bird in a central position within the frame. First place a wing, then the body and finally the second wing.

6 Use a black fine point pen to draw around the edge of the bird's body and wings, and draw an eye. Use PVA glue to attach the olive branch so it looks as though the bird is carrying it in its beak.

bookmark

This card contains both a gift and a greeting. The bookmark can be removed and will be a wonderful reminder of a birthday or special occasion.

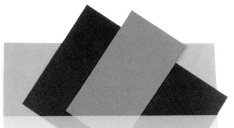

you will need

- Pattern cutting sheet
- Cutting mat
- Masking tape
- Scissors
- Mauve and pink two-tone paper
- Craft knife
- Metal ruler
- PVA glue
- Double-sided tape
- Black card
- Mauve card
- Corner cutter
- Purple dauber
- Mottled grey card
- Stylus
- Silver 3D paint
- 4 tiny green beads

timing Take your time when marking up and cutting the pattern for this card; it has to be precise.

alternative You could make a bookmark using an embossed, stamped design. Make up a base in sympathetic colours.

1 Secure the cutting sheet to a cutting mat with masking tape. Slide a 13 x 4cm (5¼ x 1½in) piece of two-tone paper under the chevron pattern and cut a line of chevrons 8.5cm (3½in) long. (If you do not have a pattern cutting sheet use the template on page 151. Trace on to acetate, then cut through the marked chevrons to create the folding areas.)

2 Fold the cut out chevrons to create the pattern and use PVA glue to hold them in place. Shape the top and bottom into points. Use double-sided tape to attach the chevron pattern centrally on a 13.5 x 4.75cm (5¼ x 1⅞in) rectangle of black card. Shape the top of the black card into a point and round the bottom corners.

3 Cut out a 14 x 6cm (5½ x 2½in) piece of mauve card. Use a corner cutter to cut out each corner. It must make a cut that will hold the bookmark in place.

4 Press a dauber around the edge of the mauve card.

5 Cut out a 16.5 x 16cm (6½ x 6¼in) piece of mottled grey card. Score and fold it in half to create the base. Use double-sided tape to attach the bookmark holder centrally on the card base.

6 Slip the bookmark in place. Put tiny dots of silver 3D paint in each corner of the mauve bookmark holder. Place a bead on each paint dot.

memories

When searching for an idea for a Mother's Day card I came across this long forgotten photograph.

I hope it inspires you to make something similar for someone special in your life.

you will need

- A4 sheet mottled brown card
- Craft knife
- Metal ruler
- Pencil
- Cutting mat
- Stylus
- Oval cutter, template and board

- A5 sheet textured cream card
- Suitable photograph
- Corner punch
- Double-sided tape
- Scissors
- A5 sheet cream paper

 **timing** Take your time when making this card; it's a gift as well as a greeting.

alternative Try the card in more modern colours if you are using a recent photograph.

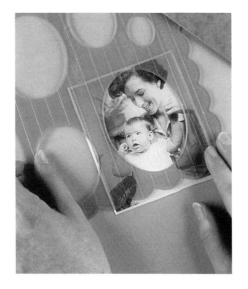

1 Cut a 21 x 13cm (8¼ x 5in) rectangle from the sheet of mottled brown card. Score and fold it in half to create the card base. Use the oval cutter, template and board to cut your photograph into a 10 x 7.5cm (4 x 3in) oval shape. If you do not have an oval cutter use the templates on page 152.

2 Cut a 10 x 12cm (4 x 4¾in) rectangle out of textured cream card. Cut a 9 x 6.5cm (3½ x 2½in) oval in a central position on the cream card. Cut a 10.5 x 7.5cm (4¼ x 3in) oval from mottled brown card and then cut a 9 x 6.5cm (3½ x 2½in) out of that. This will frame the photograph.

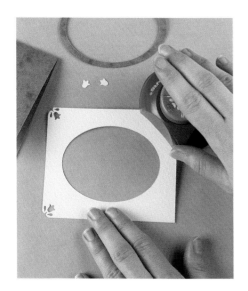

3 Use a punch to decorate each corner of the cream card. (If you do not have a corner punch you might want to trim the card with scissors and decorate it with dots of 3D paint).

4 Use double-sided tape to layer up the card. Tape the photograph in position beneath the decorated cream card and attach the frame. Stick the completed picture to the card front.

5 Cut a 20 x 11cm (8 x 4¼in) rectangle from cream paper. Fold it in half and fix in place inside the card with double-sided tape.

star surprise

No collection of cards is complete without a pop-up. This card would make a great birthday greeting for a young friend.

you will need

- A4 sheet red card
- Craft knife
- Metal ruler
- Cutting mat
- Pencil
- Stylus
- Rectangle cutter, template and board
- A5 sheet blue shimmer card
- Double-sided tape
- Scissors
- Birthday cake and parcel sequins
- Red 3D paint
- Glow in the dark star
- Silver pen
- Sheet of plasma

timing Take your time over this card as it is important to get the construction right.

alternative Once you have mastered the art of pop-up, the sky's the limit. Use different background colours and replace the star with a flower, spaceship, buzzy bee, birthday cake – anything you want!

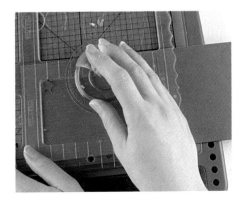

1 Cut the sheet of red card in half lengthwise. Take one piece and score and fold it in half to create the card base. Cut out a 6 x 10cm (2½ x 4in) rectangle from the front of base.

2 Cut out a 6 x 10cm (2½ x 4in) rectangle from the centre of the sheet of blue shimmer card. Cut a 1.25cm (½in) border around the rectangular hole to create a frame. Use double-sided tape to attach it to the front of the card to frame the window.

3 Use double-sided tape to attach birthday cake and parcel sequins around the frame.

4 Use 3D red paint to print a pattern of dots between the sequins. Leave to dry.

5 Tape the glow-in-the-dark star to red card. Cut around it to leave a frame. Decorate the frame using a silver pen (see photo opposite) and embellish the star with red 3D paint.

6 When the paint is dry assemble the card. Cut a strip of plasma 0.5 x 14cm (¼ x 5½in). Tape one end to the interior of the card and stick the star to the other end.

balloon magic

A perfect birthday card. Use the balloon design to decorate gift-bags and boxes. If you do not have a suitable bow button, use a fabric or string bow.

you will need

- A5 sheet of violet card
- Stylus
- Ruler
- A5 sheet green card
- Craft knife
- Cutting mat
- Pencil
- Double-sided tape
- Scissors
- Sheet spotted paper
- White card scrap
- Yellow card scrap
- Blue, red and yellow craft wire
- Super glue
- Circle cutter, template and board
- Blue and red card scraps
- 3D tape
- Bow-shaped button
- 3 tiny beads – blue, red and yellow
- Purple 3D paint

timing This card takes a while as cutting out the circles is a delicate operation.

alternative Place a bunch of cut out or punched flowers on green craft wire stalks. Tie together with a button bow and set them against a background of buzzing bee stamped paper.

1 Score and fold the sheet of violet card to create the base. Cut a 12 x 7.5cm (4¾ x 3in) piece of green card. Use double-sided tape to attach it centrally on the base. Cut an 11 x 6.5cm (4½ x 2½in) piece of spotted paper. Tape this to the green card.

2 Cut a 3 x 7.5cm (1¼ x 3in) rectangle out of white card. Attach it to a piece of yellow card and cut away all but a narrow frame. Stick these layers centrally on the spotted paper.

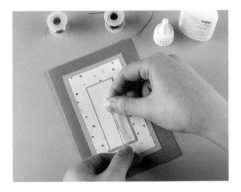

3 Cut 7cm (2¾in) of blue, red and yellow wire. Use super glue to attach a short section of the bunch of wire "strings" to the card. Allow to dry. Fan out the top and bottom of the wires.

4 Use the circle cutter, template and board to cut two 2.5cm (1in) circles from blue, red and yellow card.

5 Using double-sided tape, position the bottom layer of each balloon on the card to correspond with the same colour wire. Place the circles underneath the wires. Put 3D tape on top of the wires then put the top layers of the balloons in place.

6 Use super glue to attach the bow and the beads, and paint 3D purple dots at each corner of the green card.

kaleidoscope

People have been folding paper to create patterns for generations. Teabag

folding is an intricate system to create kaleidoscope-like effects.

you will need

- A5 sheet blue card
- Craft knife
- Metal ruler
- Pencil
- Cutting mat
- Stylus
- A5 sheet white card
- Double-sided tape
- Scissors
- A5 sheet orange card
- Sheet of decorative paper (suitable for folding)

timing You should spend some time practising your paper folding.

alternative The pattern created depends on the colours of the paper squares you use.

1 Cut a 21 x 10cm (8¼ x 4in) rectangle out of the blue card. Score and fold in half to create the card base. Cut a piece of white card 7cm (2¾in) square. Use double-sided tape to attach it to the orange card. Cut away all but a narrow frame around the white card. Use double-sided tape to attach it to the card front.

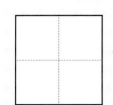 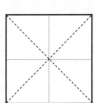

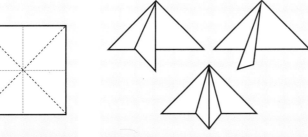

2 Cut four 5cm (2in) squares of decorative paper. Place a square of decorated paper face up on the surface. Fold in half in both directions. Fold the opened up square in half diagonally in both directions. Push in the sides to form a triangle.

3 Fold one corner towards the central fold line. Fold the corner back on itself. Make the same fold on the other side of the triangle. Open out both folds and flatten them to make the shape. Repeat with the other three squares.

4 Use double-sided tape to attach the four folded shapes to the card.

elephant trails

A wealth of history and craftsmanship has gone into creating this card. The stamp is one of many commercially available stamps handcrafted in India using traditional skills, local wood and handtools.

you will need

- A4 sheet white card
- Craft knife
- Metal ruler
- Cutting mat
- Stylus
- Aerosol glue
- Embroidered paper
- Suitable elephant stamp
- Red stamp pad
- Scrap paper

- Red sparkle embossing powder
- Tweezers or tongs
- Precision heat tool
- Pencil
- Gold pen
- Card in green, yellow, blue, red and gold
- Double-sided tape
- Scissors
- 3D double-sided tape

1 Cut the sheet of white card in half. Score and fold one half to create the card base. Spray a layer of aerosol glue on the exterior of the card base and set it aside for a minute or two to become tacky. Then lay the card base on to the reverse side of the embroidered paper. Smooth into place and cut away any excess.

2 Using your chosen stamp and the red stamp pad print a selection of images across the white card. Fold a sheet of scrap paper in half and open it out. Place the white card on to the scrap paper and sprinkle the embossing powder over the images. Shake off the excess powder and return it to the pot.

3 Holding the stamped card with tweezers or tongs, seal the embossing powder with the precision heat tool. Select the best image and use the ruler and pencil to mark up a 4 x 3cm (1½ x 1¼in) rectangle around it. Cut it out. Highlight the image with the gold pen.

4 Cut out the layers: 6.25 x 5.25cm (2½ x 2in) rectangle of red card; 5.5 x 4.5cm (2¼ x 1¾in) rectangle of blue card; 5 x 4cm (2 x 1½in) rectangle of yellow card and 4.5 x 3.5cm (1¾ x 1¼in) rectangle of green card. Use double-sided tape to attach them one on top of the other (in the order in which you cut them out) on the card base.

5 Use double-sided tape to attach the stamped and embossed elephant to a piece of gold card. Cut a narrow border around the image. Use 3D double-sided tape to attach it to the layers.

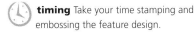

timing Take your time stamping and embossing the feature design.

alternative Traditional wooden stamps come in all shapes and sizes. Enjoy creating your own designs with handmade stamps.

coordinating items
A sheet of beautifully crafted wrapping paper can be used to make a gift-bag or to cover a gift pouch (see pages 20–21).

say it with flowers

projects

flower power

This display of paper flowers strewn across a violet card will bring a little summer magic

into someone's life.

you will need

- A5 sheet violet card
- Metal ruler
- Stylus
- Craft knife
- Cutting mat
- Pencil
- Large flower punch

- Small flower punch
- Yellow, pink, red, orange, green and blue sugar paper
- Tweezers
- PVA glue
- Pale green gel pen
- Yellow 3D paint

timing A quick and simple card to make.

alternative
Decorate a sky-blue card with punched butterflies. Replace the gel pen dots with tiny stamped daisies.

Coordinating items

Vary the background colour and try your hand at decorating a gift-box or tag using punched paper flowers. Use a flower stamp to decorate tissue paper. You might want to use embossing powder to highlight the flower petals or centres.

1 Score and fold the violet card to create the card base. Use the metal ruler and craft knife to trim the folded card to a height of 11cm (4½in).

2 Use the punches to cut out a selection of large and small flowers from sugar paper. Use PVA glue to attach small flowers centrally on large flowers.

3 Attach the prepared flowers across the card in an attractive pattern using PVA glue.

4 Use the pale green gel pen to draw small spots between the flowers. Finally, decorate each flower with a centrally placed dot of yellow 3D paint.

pink gingham

Gingham and daisies come together to create this delightfully pretty card. Cover gift-boxes with daisy-stamped gingham paper and make coordinating gift-tags.

you will need

- A5 sheet white card
- Metal ruler
- Stylus
- Aerosol glue
- Pink gingham paper
- Craft knife
- Cutting mat
- Small piece white card
- Pencil
- Four small flower rubber stamps
- Pink stamp pad
- Sheet of scrap paper
- Pink embossing powder
- Precision heat tool
- Double-sided tape
- Scissors
- Small piece dark pink card
- Pink 3D paint

timing This card is easy to make, but take care when using the embossing powder. Make sure that you cover your work surface with scrap paper.

alternative Try this design in blue or green gingham with a stamped flower feature. How about red gingham with red hearts?

1 Score and fold the sheet of white card to create the card base. Spray aerosol glue over the exterior of the card. Lay the gingham paper on to the sticky card base and smooth it down, removing any air bubbles. Trim away any excess.

3 Fold a sheet of scrap paper in half and open out. Holding the printed white square over the paper, sprinkle pink embossing powder over it. Shake off the excess powder and return to the pot.

5 Cut out four narrow 8cm (3¼in) long ribbons from the dark pink card. Use double-sided tape to attach them to the card to create a frame. The ribbons should overlap.

2 Cut a piece of white card measuring 5.5cm (2¼in) square. Using the rubber stamps and a pink ink pad, stamp four different flowers on to the square.

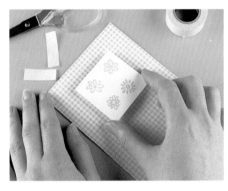

4 Seal the embossing powder with the precision heat tool. Use double-sided tape to attach the prepared flower picture in an upper central position on the front of the card.

6 Print four pink 3D paint dots, one in each corner of the frame, to give the card a professional finished look.

paper roses

As soon as I saw this lovely gift-wrap I had loads of great ideas for using it to make beautiful cards, bags and tags.

you will need

- A5 sheet pink card
- Craft knife
- Cutting mat
- Metal ruler
- Pencil
- Stylus

- Rose-patterned wrapping paper
- Double-sided tape
- Scissors
- Silver card
- Sheet of plasma
- Pink 3D paint

timing This card can be made in a matter of minutes, making it ideal to mass-produce for wedding invitations or thank-you notes.

alternative Gift-wrap with a nautical theme would be fun to use. Cut out a picture of a ship and set it against a blue backdrop.

Coordinating items *Use tissue paper to make unusual gift-bag handles: spray a thin layer of aerosol glue across a sheet of tissue paper, crinkle and roll the paper, pressing to make a length of "rope".*

1 Cut the card base out of the pink card, it should measure 21 x 10cm (8¼ x 4in). Score and fold in half. Cut an 8.75 x 8.5cm (3½ x 3¼in) rectangle from the wrapping paper. Attach it in a central position on the card base using double-sided tape.

2 Cut out a piece of silver card 7.5 x 7.25cm (3 x 2⅞in). Use double-sided tape to attach it in a central position on the rose-patterned square. Cut a piece of plasma 7 x 6.75cm (2¾ x 2⅝in) and stick this on top of the silver card.

3 Draw a box 5.5 x 5.25cm (2¼ x 2in) around a rose on the patterned paper. Cut out. Use double-sided tape to attach it centrally on the plasma.

4 Use pink 3D paint to print dots around the edge of the plasma to frame the rose.

daisy rainbow

A rainbow of daisies decorates this bright yellow card, with highlights in green and gold. For other creative ways to use a daisy punch see pages 134–35.

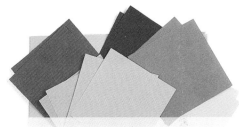

you will need

- A5 sheet yellow card
- Craft knife
- Cutting mat
- Metal ruler
- Stylus
- Gold and green pens
- Daisy punch
- Blue, red, pink and white paper
- PVA glue
- Tweezers
- Purple 3D paint

timing This card is very effective, yet extremely easy to make. Using a punch is a quick way of working.

alternative A line of randomly placed punched dragonflies set against a dark blue base would make a stunning card.

1 Cut a rectangle 21 x 10cm (8¼ x 4in) from the yellow card. Score and fold to create the card base. Open it out. Use a ruler and the green and gold pens to draw lines down the card; front and back.

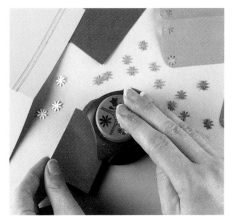

2 Punch around 20 daisies out of the coloured papers.

3 Place dots of PVA glue on and around the ruled lines. Position the daisies on the glue dots.

4 Squeeze a spot of purple 3D paint in the centre of each flower and also groups of three dots between the flowers.

Coordinating items *Have fun with your daisy punch. Use it to create wrapping paper, gift-tags, boxes and pouches.*

funky foam flowers

This stylish card is made from foam sheets that come in a wonderful array of colours

and are easy to shape, cut and stick.

you will need

- A4 sheet spring green card
- Pencil
- Craft knife
- Cutting mat
- Metal ruler
- Stylus
- Scrap paper
- Scissors
- A5 sheet blue card
- Green, blue, pink and purple foam sheets
- Double-sided tape
- Pink and purple 3D paint

 **timing** This card takes a little time to make as you need to cut the foam carefully.

alternative Make a Valentine's card with red, white and hot pink layers decorated with red hearts. Embellish with silver 3D paint.

1 Cut a rectangle 22 x 11cm (8½ x 4¼in) from the sheet of green card. Score and fold to create the card base. Trace and cut out the templates on page 153. Draw around the largest square shape on to the blue card and cut the shape out.

2 Cut the medium size square out of green foam and the small square from the blue foam. Cut out two large flowers from the pink foam, one large and one small flower from the purple foam and three leaves from the green foam.

3 Take the green card base and, using double-sided tape, attach the blue card layer, followed by the green foam layer and the blue foam layer.

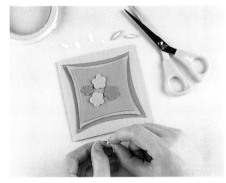

4 Use double-sided tape to attach the flower and leaf shapes. Refer to the photograph opposite for their positioning.

coordinating items *Cut out a selection of flowers and leaves from the foam sheets and use them to decorate gift-boxes and cards. You might want to try the design in a different colour scheme.*

5 Decorate the card with 3D paint using pink on the purple flowers and purple on the pink flowers and corners of the blue card.

topiary

Use rub-off transfers to create this lovely country garden scene. Once you have made the card,

try decorating a gift-box or pouch using the same motif.

you will need

- A5 sheet pink card
- Metal ruler
- Stylus
- Rectangle cutter, template and board
- Lacy pattern vellum paper
- Scissors
- Double-sided tape
- Garden motif rub-on transfers
- Transfer stick
- Green, pink and violet gel pens

timing Putting together the elements of this card takes a little time, but the finished result will bring pleasure to the recipient.

alternative Window cards are very effective. Use an interesting stamp – detailing the colour with felt-tip pens – in place of the transfer.

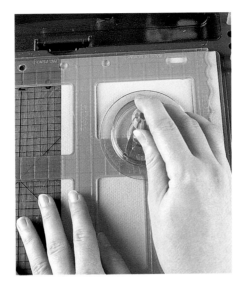

1 Score and fold the pink card to create the card base. Use the shape cutter, template and board to cut out a centrally placed 5 x 9cm (2 x 3½in) rectangle on the card front.

2 Cut two 10cm (4in) strips of vellum. Use double-sided tape to attach the strips to the interior of the card on either side of the window to give it a thin, lace border.

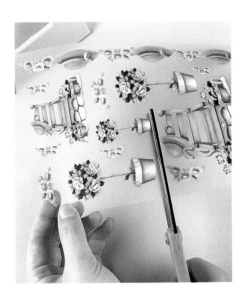

3 Cut out a suitable transfer and, following the manufacturer's instructions, transfer the design onto the interior of the card. The motif should be placed centrally so that it can be seen through the window.

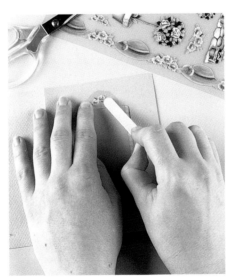

4 Apply a second transfer to the front of the card; place it centrally above the window. Use a third transfer to decorate the back of the card.

5 Frame the window with two borders using the green and pink gel pens. These can be drawn using a ruler or freehand. Complete the card by drawing little flower buds.

cherry blossom

Flower punches are so versatile. I use them all the time. This cherry blossom

covered card was inspired by pictures of spring.

you will need

- A5 sheet grey card
- Metal ruler
- Stylus
- Scissors
- Pencil
- A5 sheet silver card
- A5 sheet black card
- A5 sheet turquoise blue paper
- Double-sided tape

- Small flower punch
- Pink paper
- Marker pen
- Small piece of acetate
- Small piece brown card
- PVA glue
- Tweezers
- Silver and green 3D paints

timing Set aside an hour to make this card as there are a number of elements to prepare.

alternative Use this technique to create a Christmas card. Use a brightly coloured base and a silver frame; attach Christmas decorations to the branch.

1 Score and fold the grey card to create the card base. Cut out an 8cm (3¼in) square from silver card, a 7cm (2¾in) square from black card and a 6.5cm (2½in) square from turquoise blue card. Use double-sided tape to attach the silver square in a high central position, then stick the black and blue squares on top.

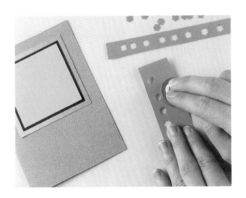

2 Your card is ready to decorate. Punch out about 22 flowers from the pink paper.

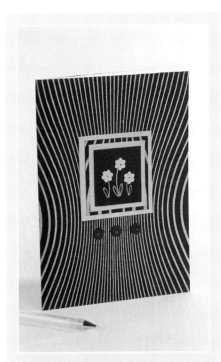

variation *This card base is gold and black gift-wrap, and the flowers punched from gold paper set against black. Use gold gel pen to draw on stems and leaves.*

3 Use the marker pen to trace the branch template on page 154 on to acetate. Cut the shape out of brown card and attach it to the front of the card using double-sided tape. The branch should look as though it is growing out of the bottom left-hand corner of the blue square.

4 Squeeze 22 dots of PVA glue where the flowers will be placed. Cherry blossom grows in clusters of three or four blooms, so bear this in mind. Place a flower on each glue dot. Attach three flowers in a row beneath the picture.

5 Place dots of green 3D paint between the flowers to resemble leaves (three or four leaves per cluster of flowers). Squeeze a dot of silver 3D paint in the centre of each flower. Don't forget to print leaves and flower centres on the flowers beneath the picture.

green blossoms

Hot orange and bright green blossoms decorate this versatile card.

Experiment with colours and produce your own designs using flower sequins.

you will need

- A5 sheet bright yellow textured card
- Metal ruler
- Stylus
- A5 sheet white card
- Craft knife
- Cutting mat
- Sheet of vellum
- Double-sided tape
- Scissors
- 3 green flower sequins
- A5 sheet orange card
- 3D adhesive tape
- Yellow 3D paint
- PVA glue
- 4 tiny green beads

timing Flower sequins are quick and easy to use.

alternative Pretty buttons set against layers of paper and card would be an interesting option.

1 Score and fold the sheet of yellow card to make the base. Cut a piece of white card 2.5 x 5.5cm (1 x 2¼in). Use double-sided tape to attach it to a vellum sheet. Use scissors to cut away all but a narrow frame around the white card.

2 Turn the white card and vellum, vellum side up and use double-sided tape to attach three green flower sequins along the length of the white card.

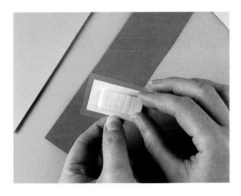

3 Attach the sequin picture to a small piece of orange card using 3D tape. Cut away all but a 4mm (⅙in) edge around the picture.

4 Use double-sided tape to attach the layers you have just assembled to white card. Cut away all but a 5mm (⅛in) frame. Then attach this to a vellum sheet; cut a 5mm (⅛in) border.

5 Use double-sided tape to attach the multi-layered picture to the orange card and cut away yet another frame of 4mm (⅙in). Finally stick the layered, framed picture in an upper central position on the front of the card using double-sided tape.

6 Put a yellow 3D paint dot in the centre of each flower. Use PVA glue to attach a green bead in each corner of the white card.

bead magic

Wirework and flower beads are framed in mint green and white to create this

pretty card. Use bead and wire designs to coordinate bags and gift-tags.

you will need

- A5 sheet of white line-embossed card
- Craft knife
- Metal ruler
- Cutting mat
- Stylus
- Pencil
- Rectangle cutter, template and board

- Small piece pale green card
- Double-sided tape
- Selection of pastel coloured beads
- Silver wire
- Wire cutters
- PVA glue
- Pink 3D paint

timing Threading and glueing the bead design for this card takes a little while.

alternative To create a Christmas card make a red frame and thread the wire with silver and clear beads and tiny stars. Scatter stars across the front of the card.

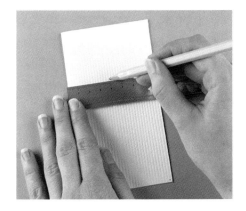

1 Cut a rectangle 16 x 15cm (6¼ x 6in) from the white card. Score and fold to make the card base. Mark up the horizontal centre of the card front, about one third of the way down.

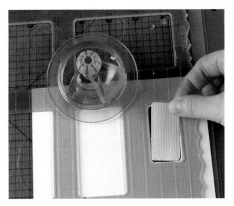

2 Using the point you have just marked as a guide, cut a 5 x 2.5cm (2 x 1in) window from the front of the card using the rectangle cutter.

3 Cut the same sized window from green card. Measure a 5mm (⅛in) border around the window and cut out.

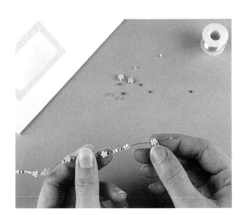

4 Use double-sided tape to attach the green frame around the window in the front of the card. Thread beads onto a length of silver wire 21cm (8¼in) long. Pinch the ends of the wire over so that the beads do not fall off.

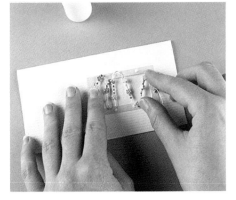

5 Shape the beaded wire into 3.5cm (1½in) zigzags. Use PVA glue to attach it to the card.

6 Mark dots in pink 3D paint along the frame. Use PVA glue to attach a single bead 5mm (⅛in) below the window.

pretty peonies

When I found these beautifully decorated paper napkins I just had to have them. Paper napkins decorated with flowers are so inspirational and pictures of peonies or roses make the most romantic greetings cards.

Use the peony napkins as gift-wrap and to decorate boxes and tags.

you will need

- 2 decorative paper napkins
- A4 sheet white card
- Craft knife
- Metal ruler
- Cutting mat
- Stylus
- Aerosol glue

- A4 white paper
- Pencil
- Small piece green card
- Small piece pink card
- Small piece white card
- Double-sided tape

timing Once you have mastered the method this card is quick and simple to make; a good design for mass-production.

alternative Make up this card in yellow and white daisies for a country feel.

1 Take the table napkins and separate the patterned layer from the remaining tissue layers. You will use the patterned layer to decorate your card. Discard the other layers.

2 Cut out a 21 x 10cm (8¼ x 4in) rectangle from white card. Score and fold to make the card base. Spray the card base with aerosol glue and position it on the back of the patterned tissue layer. Turn over and carefully smooth the tissue on to the card base. Trim away the excess tissue paper.

3 Spray the A4 sheet of white paper with aerosol glue. Smooth the second patterned tissue layer over it to attach firmly.

4 Take the decorated paper sheet and use a pencil and ruler to mark up a 4.5cm (1¾in) square. Cut out with a craft knife.

5 Cut a 6cm (2½in) square from green card, a 5.5cm (2¼in) square from pink card and a 5cm (2in) square from white card. Use double-sided tape to attach the peony decorated square centrally on the white square.

6 Layer this on to the pink square and then finally the green square. Use double-sided tape to attach the layered design centrally on the card.

special occasions

projects

patchwork house

This heart-warming little card is made from scraps of floral patchwork fabric.

A perfect way to wish friends good luck in their new home.

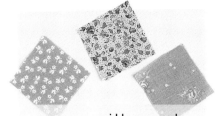

you will need

- A5 sheet pink textured card
- Metal ruler
- Craft knife
- Cutting mat
- Pencil
- Stylus
- Tracing paper
- 4 scraps of patchwork fabric
- Scissors
- Aerosol glue
- Green gel pen
- 3D pink paint

timing Once you've gathered together the scraps of fabric, this card is quick to make.

alternative Try a fabric collage in bright modern colours for a more stylish look. You could even try a paper collage.

1 Measure and cut out a rectangle 16 x 12cm (6¼ x 4¾in) from the pink card. Score and fold in half to create the base.

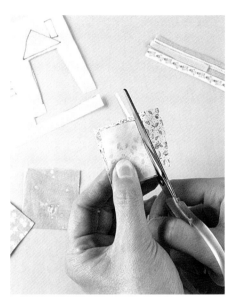

2 Trace the house template on page 154 and cut out the various shapes from your chosen fabrics.

coordinating items Construct a gift-bag using suitable wrapping paper. Decorate it with a fabric collage to coordinate with your card, along with a gift-tag.

3 Use aerosol glue to attach the fabric pieces on the card to form the house. The house should be in a lower central position.

4 Add details to the windows and door using the green gel pen. Complete the card by painting five pink 3D paint dots coming out of the chimney.

girl's best friend

Craft gems look great on cards. Here I have combined faux diamonds with silver thread and red hearts to create a modern yet romantic look, perfect for Valentine's Day or an anniversary.

you will need

- Red oven-bake clay
- Mini rolling pin
- Board
- Clingfilm
- Heart cutter
- Baking tray
- Stylus
- Ruler

- A5 sheet white textured card
- Double-sided tape
- Scissors
- Silver thread
- A5 white paper
- Super glue
- Tweezers
- Faux diamond

timing This card is very easy to make but you will need to set aside a little time as you have to bake the clay.

alternative Tiny stars and a faux jewel would create a stunning card to send best wishes to someone or even for a Christmas greeting.

1 Soften a small piece of red oven-bake clay and roll out between two layers of clingfilm. Cut out a dozen or so tiny red hearts and bake according to the manufacturer's instructions.

2 Score and fold the white card to create the card base. Place three strips of double-sided tape horizontally on the inside of the card front. One at the top, one in the middle and one at the bottom.

3 Wind silver thread around the card making sure it has a firm grip on the double-sided tape. Check the silver thread pattern you are creating on the card front as you go.

4 Attach with double-sided tape an insert of white paper cut slightly smaller than the card.

5 Use super glue to attach the red hearts to the card. Use double-sided tape to stick the faux diamond in place.

bunch of hearts

Wirework can be very effective. I have framed the wire design with tissue paper. Decorate bright

pink tissue paper with gold dots to make gift-wrap and use the card design to make gift-tags.

you will need

- A5 sheet cream textured card
- Metal ruler
- Craft knife
- Cutting mat
- Stylus
- Pink tissue paper
- Aerosol glue
- Yellow paper
- Blue paper
- Double-sided tape
- Scissors
- Red, yellow, blue and pink craft wire
- Wooden dowel
- Super glue
- Gold 3D paint

timing This card takes a little time to make but is well worth the effort.

alternative Cut snowflakes out of tissue paper. Use aerosol glue to attach them to a card base then embellish with 3D paint.

1 Use a craft knife to cut a 10.5 x 21cm (4 x 8¼in) rectangle from the cream card. Score and fold to form the base. Tear a piece of bright pink tissue paper approx. 8.5cm (3½in) square. Use aerosol glue to attach it in a central position on the front of the card.

2 Cut and assemble the layers (using double-sided tape) for the central motif in this order: a 5.5cm (2¼in) square of yellow paper, a 5cm (2in) square of blue paper and a 4.5cm (1¾in) square of cream card. Attach the layers centrally on the pink square.

3 Wind a length of red wire around a dowel three times and then stretch out a length of 10cm (4in). Cut off. Slide the wire off the dowel and press the coils together.

4 Measure 3cm (1¼in) up from the coils and make a circle of wire 1cm (½in) in diameter. Wind the excess wire around the stem. Press the top of the circle in to create a heart shape. Trim excess wire. Make hearts in blue and yellow wire as well. Use super glue to attach the hearts on the cream card.

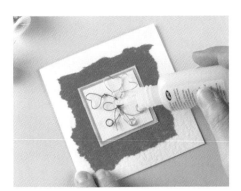

5 Cut a 6cm (2½in) length of pink wire. Make two loops then twist into a bow shape. Trim and fix in position with super glue.

6 Use 3D gold paint to outline and decorate the pink tissue paper. You could put a pink tissue paper or wire heart on the back of the card for an extra touch.

sparkling hearts

This is a romantic card perfect for sending Christmas wishes to a loved one.

These glittery hearts would look good on gift-wrap and tags too.

you will need

- Sheet cream handmade textured paper
- Craft knife
- Metal ruler
- Cutting mat
- Pencil
- Stylus
- Sheet red handmade paper
- Double-sided tape
- Scissors
- Sheet white textured card
- Sheet white line-embossed paper
- Gold glitter glue
- Acetate
- Glue stick
- Sheet pink glitter paper

 timing Set aside half an hour to make this card.

alternative A single heart would look good layered on a selection of handmade papers and set in the centre of a square card base.

1 Cut a 17 x 18cm (6¾ x 7in) shape from the cream paper. Score and fold in half to make the card base. Tear a rectangle 16.5 x 7cm (6½ x 2¾in) from the red paper. Use double-sided tape to attach it in a central position to the card front.

2 Cut a 15 x 6cm (6 x 2½in) rectangle from the white textured card. Attach it in a central position on the red paper with double-sided tape.

3 Tear out three 4.5 x 5cm (1¾ x 2in) pieces of white line-embossed paper. Edge the torn pieces with gold glitter glue and set aside to dry.

4 Trace the template on page 154. Use it to cut three heart shapes from the red paper. Use a glue stick to attach them to the pink glitter paper. Cut around each heart shape leaving a narrow border of pink glitter paper.

5 Glue the hearts on to the gold-edged torn white paper pieces to create the motifs. Using double-sided tape, attach the central motif to the card, then position the other two.

roses are red

A sheet of angel hair paper and a bunch of red paper rosebuds were used to create this beautiful card. To create a wonderful birthday card use pink roses and pink paper instead. For further ideas on using paper rosebuds, see pages 140–41.

you will need

- A5 sheet pink card
- Metal ruler
- Stylus
- Sheet white translucent paper
- Sheet angel hair paper
- Craft knife
- Cutting mat
- Double-sided tape
- Scissors
- Sheet red handmade paper
- Small piece green card
- Small piece white card
- 2 paper rosebuds
- Gold yarn
- PVA glue
- 2 red heart sequins

timing Once the shapes are cut out this card takes no time to make at all.

alternative To make a simple but unique card, attach a small bunch of silk lily of the valley to a sage green card base.

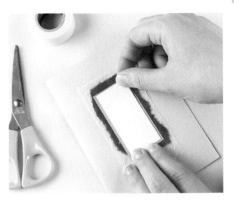

1 Score and fold the sheet of pink card to create the card base. Measure and cut out rectangles of white translucent and angel hair paper, 10.5 x 5.5cm (4¼ x 2¼in). Use double-sided tape to attach the white translucent paper in a central position on the card base. Stick the angel hair paper on top.

2 Tear an 8 x 4.5cm (3¼ x 1¾in) rectangle from the red handmade paper. Cut a 7 x 3.5cm (2¾ x 1½in) rectangle from the green card and a 6.5 x 3cm (2½ x 1¼in) rectangle from the white card. Using double-sided tape, layer the red paper, the green card and finally the white card onto the angel hair paper.

3 Tie the two rosebud stems together with a 10cm (4in) length of gold yarn. Use PVA glue to attach firmly in place on the card.

4 Trim the ends of the yarn to about 2cm (¾in) in length. Use double-sided tape to attach the red heart sequins to the ends of the yarn.

coordinating items

Gift-tags decorated with paper flowers look lovely attached to a birthday posy. Get hold of a bunch of paper flowers and experiment with backgrounds and layers.

wedding cake

A confection in candy pink, crisp white and subtle silver with which to send wedding or anniversary greetings. Use the cake motif to decorate boxes and pouches. These could be used for wedding favours.

you will need

- Sheet A4 white textured card
- Craft knife
- Metal ruler
- Cutting mat
- Stylus
- A5 sheet pink card
- Double-sided tape
- Scissors
- Sheet of plasma
- Silver and white 3D paint
- Acetate
- Marker pen
- Pink gel pen
- Silver pen
- Silver card
- Silver wire
- Pencil
- Silver heart sequin
- PVA glue
- Hole punch
- Thin white ribbon

timing The sophisticated simplicity of this card takes a little while to achieve.

alternative Make this card up in lemon yellow and replace the cake with a silver stork peel-off to make a delightful newborn baby card.

1 Cut out a 16 x 15cm (6½ x 6in) piece of white textured card. Score and fold in half to create the card base. Measure and cut out a 14 x 6cm (5½ x 2½in) rectangle from the pink card. Use double-sided tape to attach it in a central position on the card base.

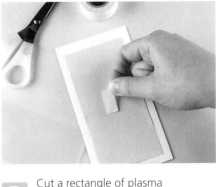

2 Cut a rectangle of plasma measuring 5.5 x 12.5cm (2¼ x 5in). Use double-sided tape to attach it in a central position. Ensure that the tape is centrally placed on the plasma so it remains invisible on the finished card. Place a silver 3D paint spot in each corner of the plasma.

3 Trace the templates on page 154 on to acetate. Cut out of white textured card. Draw a pink scallop pattern along the upper edges of the cake layers. Use silver pen to colour in the cake boards along the lower edges of the cake layers.

4 Cut four narrow ribbons of silver card, 1cm (½in) in length. These will make the cake stands. Cut two lengths of silver wire 8cm (3¼in) long. Make a curl in the end of each length of wire by wrapping them around a pencil.

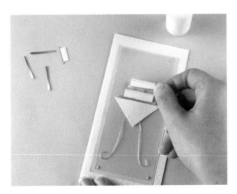

5 Use double-sided tape to assemble the card. Begin by laying the wire table legs in place. Attach the remaining pieces from the bottom up. Glue the heart sequin in place and decorate the tablecloth with a border of white 3D dots.

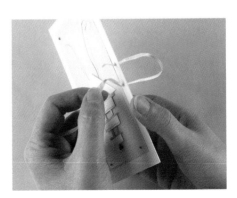

6 Use a hole punch to make two holes on the left side of the card. Thread white ribbon through the holes and tie a bow.

turtle-doves

Pretty cake ribbon is used to decorate this wedding card. Visit your local cake decorating store; you'll find plenty to inspire your greetings card creativity.

you will need

- A4 sheet white card
- Stylus
- Metal ruler
- Craft knife
- Cutting mat
- Aerosol glue

- White heart-decorated mulberry paper
- A5 sheet gold card
- Double-sided tape
- Scissors
- Decorative ribbon 5 cm (2in) wide

timing This card is easy to make and can be quickly mass-produced, making it an ideal wedding invitation.

alternative Make this card up in bright colours and use a length of nursery ribbon for an unusual birthday greeting.

variation *The mulberry paper used for this card makes a great base for a variety of cards and tags. The double hearts were purchased from a cake decorating shop.*

1 Cut the sheet of white card in half. Score and fold one half to create the base. Spray aerosol glue on the outside of the card base. Lay this on top of the mulberry paper. Smooth the paper over the card and use a craft knife to cut away the excess from around the card blank.

2 Cut a piece of gold card, 10 x 6cm (4 x 2½in) and a piece of white card, 9.5 x 5.5cm (3¾ x 2¼in). Use double-sided tape to layer them centrally on the card base.

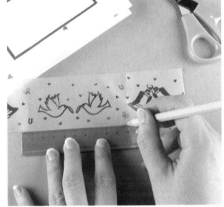

3 Measure and cut a 9cm (3½in) length of ribbon. Be sure to cut it so that the image is in the centre of the piece of ribbon.

4 Use aerosol glue to attach the ribbon centrally on the white card creating a framed picture.

tiny togs

I love this card. To me it is everything a new arrival card should be – simple, pretty and unbelievably cute.

you will need

- Small piece white textured card
- Deckle-edge scissors
- Pencil
- Metal ruler
- Blue and yellow 3D paint
- Suitable cut-out of baby outfit
- Acetate
- Marker pen
- Blue foam sheet scrap
- Scissors

- Small length of gold craft wire
- Double-sided tape
- 3D tape
- A5 sheet baby blue card
- A5 sheet white card
- A5 sheet blue gingham paper
- A5 sheet yellow card
- Large and small flower punches
- PVA glue

timing Set aside a quiet hour to make this special greetings card.

alternative Three-dimensional cards are very effective. Cut-outs which represent a hobby or interest would look good when used in this way.

coordinating items *This design works well in pink as well as blue. You can make an array of items to match the card including gift-bags, tags and lined envelopes (see page 18).*

1 Use the deckle-edge scissors to cut a 5 x 7.5cm (2 x 3in) rectangle from the sheet of white textured card. Edge with a line of blue 3D paint. Leave to dry.

2 Cut out a baby outfit and back it if necessary. Trace the coathanger template on page 154. Construct using the foam sheet and wire. Use double-sided tape to attach it to the sheet of blue deckle-edged card. Use 3D tape to attach the baby outfit giving the impression it is hanging up.

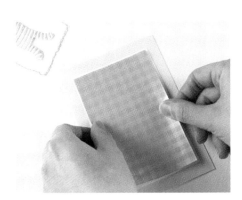

3 Score and fold the sheet of baby blue card to create the card base. Cut a 12.5 x 8cm (5 x 3¼in) rectangle of white card and a 12 x 7.5cm (4¾ x 3in) rectangle of gingham paper. Attach the white card using double-sided tape and the gingham paper using aerosol glue, in a central position on the base.

4 Cut out a 9 x 6.5cm (3½ x 2½in) rectangle of yellow card. Use double-sided tape to attach it in an upper central position on the gingham paper and finally stick the baby outfit motif on top of that.

5 Punch out one large and two small flowers from the white card. Use 3D tape to stick the large flower underneath the motif. Glue the two small flowers either side of it. Paint yellow 3D centres in each flower and in the corners of the framed picture.

baby carriage

A sheet of beautiful gift-wrap inspired this traditional new baby card. Use other motifs on the paper to decorate the envelope.

These different, but equally pretty, designs can be created using more modern images.

you will need

- A5 sheet cream textured card
- Metal ruler
- Stylus
- Sheet suitable wrapping paper
- Scissors
- Sheet green translucent paper
- Craft knife
- Cutting mat
- Aerosol glue
- Sheet mottled buff paper
- Double-sided tape

timing This card couldn't be more simple. It can be made and in the post in a matter of minutes.

alternative Use a silver peel-off baby motif and decorate the card with silver flowers for a stylish option.

1 Score and fold the cream textured card to make the card blank. Use sharp scissors to cut around your chosen image. The image should be approximately 6.5cm (2½in) square.

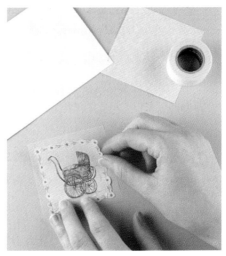

2 Cut an 8cm (3¼in) square of green translucent paper. Use aerosol glue to attach the image to it. Cut an 8.5cm (3½in) square of mottled buff paper and use double-sided tape to attach the green-framed image to it. Stick the framed picture in an upper central position on the card front.

3 Use another small cut-out to decorate the card. Use double-sided tape to stick it beneath the framed picture.

4 Give the card a professional finish by sticking a tiny cut-out in a low central position on the back of the card.

coordinating items *You can make other items to match your card that aren't decorated with actual motifs from the wrapping paper, merely inspired by it. For example, here I have picked up on the daisy pattern from the paper and used a daisy rubber stamp and punch to decorate a bag, a box and wrapping papers.*

rocking horse

This framed rocking horse makes a lovely card. It would be wonderful to use for baby announcement cards or thank-you notes for new baby gifts.

you will need

- A5 sheet white textured card
- Metal ruler
- Stylus
- Sheet pink card
- Craft knife
- Cutting mat

- Double-sided tape
- Sheet white card
- Sheet silver card
- Peel-off sticker
- Embossing board and heart template
- Pink 3D paint

timing Peel-offs are very quick and easy to use so this is a good card to mass-produce.

alternative A photograph of a baby set on a blue or pink background would make a cute card.

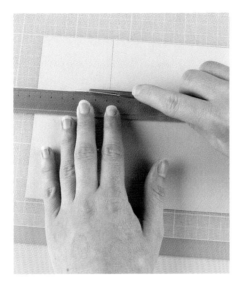

1 Score and fold the white textured card to create the base. Cut a piece of pink card 6.5 x 5cm (2½ x 2in). Use double-sided tape to attach it to a sheet of white card.

2 Cut away all but a narrow frame around the pink card. Use double-sided tape to attach it to silver card. Once again cut away all but a narrow border.

3 Stick the peel-off centrally on the frame. Use double-sided tape to attach the framed image in an upper central position on the card front.

4 Using the embossing board and template, emboss a small heart shape in a central position below the framed picture.

5 Use pink 3D paint to mark a dot in each corner, slightly outside the frame, to complete the card.

teddy bear

New arrival cards are always a pleasure to make and this card is particularly special with the ribbon and rivet design. Ring the changes with a pink, lemon yellow or green background and use other peel-offs to decorate bags, tags and boxes.

you will need

- A4 sheet white textured card
- Craft knife
- Metal ruler
- Cutting mat
- Stylus
- Pencil
- Wooden board
- Rivet setting tools
- Hammer
- 6 silver rivets

- Small piece pale blue card
- Double-sided tape
- Scissors
- Small piece silver card
- Silver teddy bear peel-off
- Silver heart sequin
- PVA glue
- Thin pale blue ribbon

timing You need to spend a little time on this card as it is important to get the rivets positioned evenly and neatly.

alternative Turn this card into a wedding invitation – use a suitable peel-off to replace the teddy and insert printed invitation details.

1 Cut the sheet of white card in half. Score and fold one half to make the card base. Measure in 1cm (½in) from the folded edge of the card. Working down the card, mark light pencil dots at 1.5cm (½in), 4cm (1½in), 6.5cm (2½in), 8.5cm (3¼in), 11cm (4¼in) and 13.5cm (5¼in).

2 Place the card on a wooden board. Use the rivet hole maker and a hammer to make holes at the marked spots.

3 Press the rivets through the holes. Use a hammer and the rivet placement tool to secure the rivet.

4 Cut out a 4 x 3.5cm (1½ x 1¼in) rectangle from pale blue card. Use double-sided tape to attach this to a piece of textured white card. Cut away all but a narrow frame. Tape this on to silver card and cut away all but a narrow frame.

5 Attach the layers in an upper central position on the card front. Place the teddy bear peel-off sticker in a central position on the blue card. Glue a small silver heart 1cm (½in) beneath the framed picture.

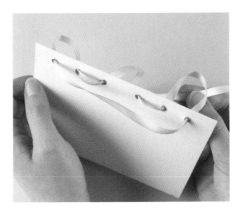

6 Thread the blue ribbon through the rivets and tie a bow.

witches abroad

I have used a selection of Hallowe'en-themed collage stickers on this card. If you cannot find suitable stickers or want to be even more creative, try creating your own collages using stickers and coloured paper.

you will need

- A5 sheet black card
- Craft knife
- Metal ruler
- Cutting mat
- Stylus
- Black glitter card
- Double-sided tape
- Scissors
- Lime green card
- Yellow card
- Hallowe'en collage stickers
- Gold 3D paint
- Star stickers

 **timing** This card is quick to make if you use bought collages.

alternative Try a freehand drawing of a scary spider decorated with 3D paint for a simple card.

1 Cut a 15 x 11cm (6 x 4½in) rectangle from the black card. Score and fold to create the card base. Prepare the motifs. Cut a 2.5cm (1in) square from the black glitter card. Use double-sided tape to attach the square to lime green card. Cut away all but a narrow border. Then stick this to yellow card and again, cut away all but a narrow border. Repeat this process to make a second motif.

2 Use double-sided tape to stick the collage stickers in position on the motifs. Place the central sticker on the card first and then the two motifs.

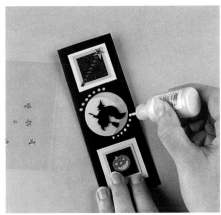

3 Use gold 3D paint to print dots around the central sticker – seven on the upper left and ten on the lower right.

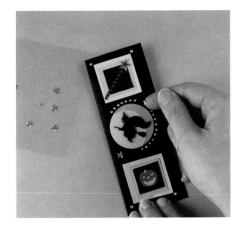

4 Print gold dots on the upper corners of the top motif and the lower corners of the bottom motif. Lay two stars decoratively on the upper right and lower left of the central sticker.

coordinating items
Decorate goodie bags with motifs and stars. Wrap gifts in corrugated card and make tags using single motifs.

happy hallowe'en

Celebrate Hallowe'en with this collage card. The card is made up of many elements – freehand drawing, rubber stamping and paper cut-outs. You can create many designs using a collage of different materials. Try using stickers as well.

you will need

- A4 sheet black card
- Craft knife
- Metal ruler
- Cutting mat
- Stylus
- Pencil
- Double-sided tape
- Scissors
- Sheet black glitter card

- Green, pink, white and blue gel pens
- Acetate
- Sheet white card
- PVA glue
- 2 tiny boggle eyes
- Sheet orange card
- Black fine liner pen
- Frog rubber stamp
- Green stamp pad

timing Take same time to practise your freehand drawing before you start making the card.

alternative Personalize a card with a photo of someone in fancy dress.

1 Cut the A4 sheet of black card in half. Score and fold one half to create the card base. Cut a rectangle of black card 7 x 10cm (2¾ x 4in). Use double-sided tape to attach it to a sheet of glitter card. Cut away all but a narrow border. Use double-sided tape to attach it centrally on the card base.

2 Draw a white gel pen spider web in the top right-hand corner of the card. Draw a spider in the centre.

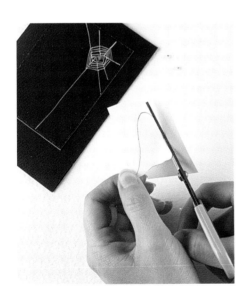

3 Trace the ghostly shape on page 154 and cut it out of white card. Use PVA glue to attach two boggle eyes. Tape the ghost in the top left-hand corner of the card.

4 Trace the pumpkin templates on page 154 and cut out in orange card. Draw lines on using a black fine liner pen to give them more shape.

5 Stamp a green frog on to the bottom right-hand corner of the card and use a blue gel pen to draw three ripples around it.

magic number

Number cut-outs make great card decorations. This card will work with any number and there

are templates for numbers 0–9 on pages 156–57. If the number you want to use is in double figures,

simply reduce the size of the numbers and overlap them slightly on the card.

you will need

- A5 sheet spring green card
- Metal ruler
- Stylus
- Yellow card
- Cutting mat
- Craft knife
- Pencil
- Double-sided tape
- Scissors
- Red card

- Blue corrugated card
- Yellow and blue 3D paint
- Tracing paper/ acetate
- Spotty wrapping paper
- White paper
- 3D tape
- Spring green paper

1 Score and fold the green card to create the card blank. Cut out a 10 x 8cm (4 x 3in) rectangle from the yellow card. Attach it to the card blank in an upper central position using double-sided tape.

 timing Take your time cutting out the number as the other elements of this card are quick and easy to put together.

alternative The sky's the limit – use different wrapping papers to create different effects.

coordinating items
Number motifs brighten up plain white or brown bags wonderfully. I created the handle of the smaller bag using an oval cutter, template and board.

2 Cut out a 9.5 x 7.5cm (3¾ x 3in) rectangle from the red card. Tape it on top of the yellow card. Cut out an 8.5 x 6.5cm (3½ x 2½in) rectangle of blue corrugated card. Attach this to the red card.

3 Use yellow and blue 3D paint to mark a dotty border on the red frame. Trace the number template on page 156 or 157. Cut the figure out of the wrapping paper. (If you are using translucent gift-wrap back it with a sheet of white copy paper before cutting out.)

4 Use 3D tape to attach the number to a sheet of green paper. Cut around the number to create a narrow border. Use double-sided tape to attach the number centrally on the card.

projects

chick chick chicken

This card is decorated with an interesting button. For spring greetings mint green and yellow are

a lovely colour combination. Look around for other motifs or buttons that would look good with

these colours.

you will need

- A5 sheet pale green card
- Metal ruler
- Stylus
- Sheet white corrugated card
- Craft knife
- Cutting mat
- Chicken button
- 3D tape

- Sheet dotty paper
- Double-sided tape
- Scissors
- Sheet yellow translucent paper
- Sheet green translucent paper
- Daisy punch
- PVA glue
- Yellow 3D paint

timing Set aside an afternoon to make Easter cards for your friends.

alternative Look out for interesting buttons and coordinate them with suitable bases.

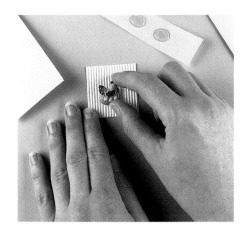

1 Score and fold the pale green card to create the card base. Cut a 4.5cm (1¾in) square of white corrugated card. Use 3D tape to attach the button in a central position on the square.

2 Cut a 6.5cm (2½in) square from dotty paper. Use double-sided tape to attach the motif in a central position on the dotty paper.

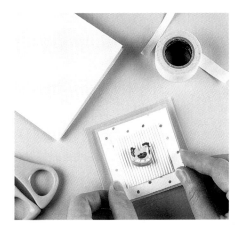

3 Use double-sided tape to attach the framed motif to a sheet of yellow translucent paper. Cut away all but a narrow frame. Tape this to a sheet of 8cm (3¼in) square of green translucent paper.

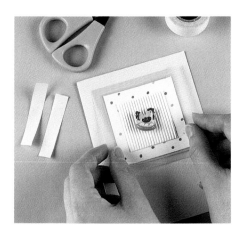

4 Attach the layered picture in an upper central position on the green card base.

5 Punch out three white daisies and use PVA glue to attach them in a row beneath the picture.

6 Put dots of 3D paint in the corners of the framed picture and in the centre of each daisy.

easter bunnies

Use paper table napkins and wooden cut-outs to make this greetings card. If you cannot find wooden motifs use stickers or make your own paper cut-outs to achieve a similar effect.

you will need

- A4 sheet yellow card
- Metal ruler
- Pencil
- Craft knife
- Cutting mat
- Stylus
- A5 sheet green card
- Double-sided tape
- Scissors

- A5 sheet orange card
- Sheet yellow translucent paper
- A5 sheet white card
- 3 wooden rabbit cut-outs
- Easter paper napkin
- White paper
- Aerosol glue
- Green 3D paint

timing Preparing the elements of this card takes a little time.

alternative Make a card with a nautical theme – use sailboat motifs.

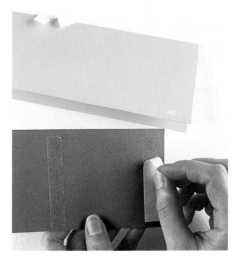

1 Cut a 19.5 x 16cm (7¾ x 6in) rectangle from yellow card. Score and fold it in half so that the card base is landscape. Cut a 19 x 7cm (7½ x 2¾in) rectangle of green card and use double-sided tape to attach it to the card base. Cut a 18.5 x 6.5cm (7¼ x 2½in) rectangle of orange card. Use double-sided tape to attach it centrally on the green card.

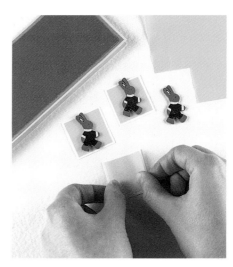

2 Measure and cut out three 3.5cm (1¼in) squares of yellow translucent paper and three 3.75cm (1½in) squares of white card. Use double-sided tape to attach the yellow squares to the white squares. Tape the rabbit motifs centrally on each yellow square.

3 Separate the decorated layer of the napkin from the other layers. Spray a sheet of white paper with aerosol glue and smooth the napkin on to it. Cut out four eggs.

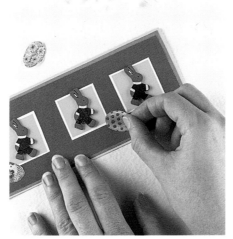

4 Use double-sided tape to attach the three motifs (position the central one first) and the eggs.

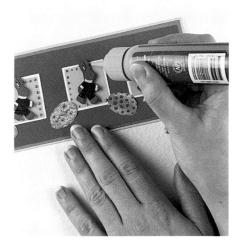

5 Paint a border of tiny dots around the yellow translucent paper squares.

nest egg

Three pretty Easter eggs in a delicate, gold wire nest adorn this card. I have used embossed stamped images to make the Easter eggs. If you don't have a stamp, cut out small ovals and decorate them with felt-tips or coloured foil. Use the decorated eggs to make alternative cards and gift-tags.

you will need

- A5 sheet blue card
- Craft knife
- Cutting mat
- Pencil
- Metal ruler
- Stylus
- A5 sheet textured white card
- Corner punch
- Blue and white polka dot paper
- Double-sided tape
- Scissors
- Gold card

- Decorative gold wire
- Super glue
- Embossing pad
- Small Easter egg rubber stamp
- Scrap of white card
- Scrap paper
- Gold embossing powder
- Tweezers or tongs
- Precision heat tool
- Felt-tip pens
- 3D tape

timing Spend a little time preparing the Easter eggs as they are the feature of the card.

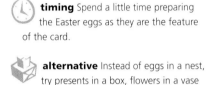

alternative Instead of eggs in a nest, try presents in a box, flowers in a vase or cakes on a plate.

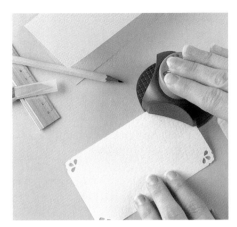

1 Cut a 16 x 13.5cm (6¼ x 5¼in) rectangle from the blue card. Score and fold to create the card base. Cut a 7 x 12.5cm (2¾ x 5in) rectangle from the white textured card. Use the corner punch to cut decorative corners.

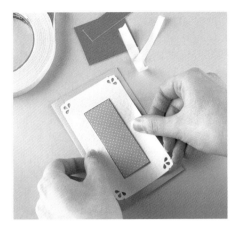

2 Cut out a 7.5 x 2.5cm (3 x 1in) rectangle from the polka dot paper. Use double-sided tape to attach it to gold card. Cut away all but a narrow border. Use double-sided tape to attach the gold-framed polka dot paper in a central position on the white textured card and then tape the layers on to the card base.

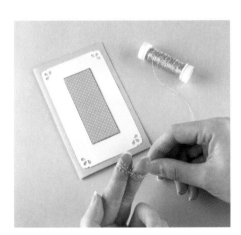

3 Make the nest by wrapping decorative gold wire around two fingers. Wrap the wire around about 10 times. Remove the wire from your fingers, cut and wrap the ends around the wire oval. Shape into a flattened nest. Glue in place with super glue.

4 Use the embossing pad and stamp to print three eggs on to a scrap of white card. Fold a sheet of scrap paper in half and open it out. Put the stamped white card on to the scrap paper and sprinkle it with gold embossing powder. Shake the excess powder on to the scrap paper and return it to the container. Holding the card with tweezers or tongs, seal the designs with the precision heat tool.

5 Use felt-tip pens to decorate the embossed eggs and cut them out. Place 3D tape on to the backs of the eggs and press in place in the nest.

easter eggs

Delicate spring flowers and pretty ribbon are the main features of this lovely Easter

card. You might want to use a different colour scheme, maybe pink and green or powder

blue and white with lemon yellow features.

you will need

- A5 sheet lilac card
- Stylus
- Metal ruler
- Oval cutter, template and board
- A5 sheet yellow and lilac spotted paper

- A4 sheet white paper
- Double-sided tape
- 7cm (2¾in) length of 1.75cm (¾in) wide pale blue organza ribbon
- 8.5cm (3¼in) of 1cm (⅜in) wide pink organza ribbon

- Aerosol glue
- Lilac blue blossom decorated paper
- Craft knife
- Cutting mat
- 3D tape
- Flower punch
- Scrap of lilac paper

- PVA glue
- Scrap of yellow paper
- Yellow and blue 3D paints

timing This card is very simple to make, but it does take a little time to assemble all the layers.

alternative Instead of an egg, wrap a Christmas present with ribbon and decorate with gold stars. Use festive wrapping paper for the layers.

1 Score and fold the lilac card to create the base. To make the egg, use the oval cutter, template and board to cut 7.5 x 5.5cm (3 x 2¼in) ovals from the spotted and the white paper. If you do not have an oval cutter use the template on page 151.

2 Attach a length of double-sided tape across the centre of the back of the spotted egg. Place the blue ribbon across the front of the egg, fold the edges around and attach them to the double-sided tape on the reverse. Attach the pink ribbon over the blue.

3 Spray aerosol glue on to one side of the white oval, attach this to the reverse of the spotted egg, this will help hold the ribbon in position and give the egg some substance. Set aside.

4 Cut a 7.5 x 9.5cm (3 x 3¾in) rectangle from the blossom paper. Use double-sided tape to attach it to spotted paper; cut away all but a narrow border. Layer this on to white paper and, once again, cut away all but a narrow border.

5 Use double-sided tape to attach this in an upper central position on the card base. Use 3D tape to attach the egg in a central position on the layers.

6 Punch out seven small flowers from lilac paper. Use PVA glue to attach three flowers across the centre of the pink ribbon and one in each corner of the frame. Punch out a yellow flower and glue beneath the layers. Squeeze a dot of yellow 3D paint on to each lilac flower and a blue 3D paint dot on to the yellow flower.

christmas trees

A stylish Christmas card made from simply decorated paper napkins.

you will need

- A5 sheet white card
- Craft knife
- Cutting mat
- Metal ruler
- Pencil
- Stylus
- Decorative paper napkin
- Aerosol glue

- A5 sheet white paper
- Scissors
- Double-sided tape
- Small piece red card
- Small piece green card
- Black fine point pen

timing This card is reasonably quick to make so it would be efficient to mass-produce.

alternative For a less seasonal look try this design using a different multi-image paper napkin, perhaps tiny flowers or balloons?

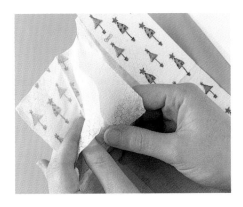

1 Cut a rectangle 20.5 x 11.5cm (8 x 4½in) from the white card. Score and fold to create the card blank. Take the napkin and separate out the patterned layer. Discard the plain layers.

2 Spray the reverse of the patterned layer with aerosol glue. Smooth it over the front of the card base and cut away the excess. Set aside. Stick the excess of the patterned layer on to a sheet of white paper. Smooth to attach firmly.

3 Cut out a single tree to be the focal point of your card. Use double-sided tape to attach the feature to a piece of red card. Cut away all but a narrow frame.

4 Use double-sided tape to attach the framed image to white card. Cut a 4.5 x 6cm (2¼ x 1¾in) rectangle. Cut a 6.3 x 7.3cm (2½ x 2¾in) rectangle of green card and attach the motif to it. Attach this to red card and cut a narrow frame.

coordinating items *Here is a set of seasonal stationery. I've used the central motif on different coloured blanks and layers. You can also use napkins as gift-wrap.*

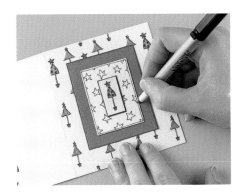

5 Attach the layered motif to the card base. Draw a black line around the edge of the white card. Add small stars. You might want to attach a small feature to the back of the card to finish it off.

hark the herald angels

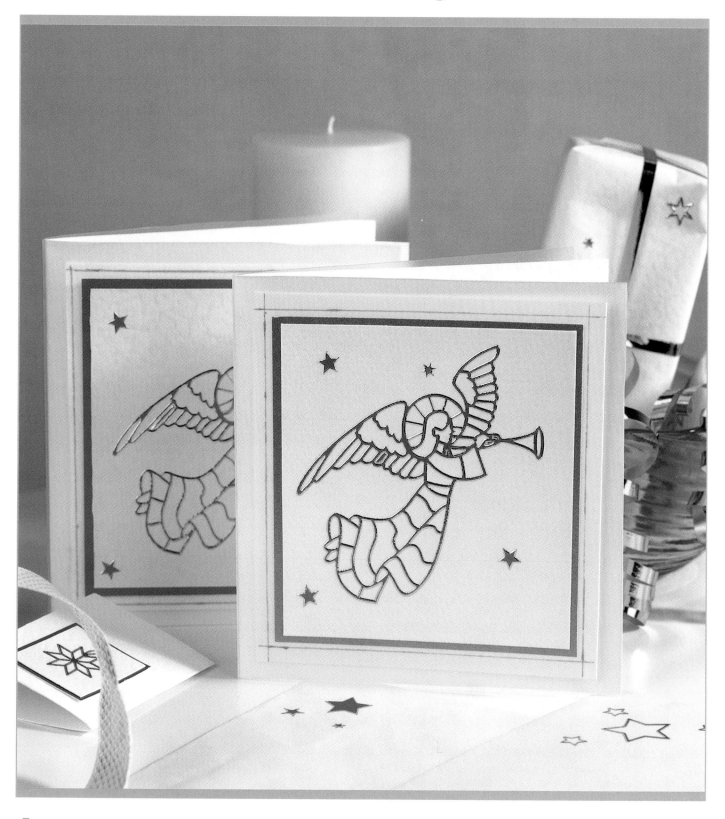

A sophisticated seasonal card using gold peel-off stickers, cream parchment and textured paper.

you will need

- A4 sheet cream textured paper
- Craft knife
- Metal ruler
- Pencil
- Cutting mat
- A4 sheet plasma
- Stylus
- Double-sided tape
- Scissors
- A5 sheet cream parchment paper
- A5 sheet gold card
- A5 sheet cream textured card
- Gold pen
- Angel peel-off sticker
- Gold star stickers

1 Cut out a 24.5 x 13cm (9½ x 5in) rectangle of cream textured paper and plasma. Score and fold the paper and the plasma.

2 Place two strips of double-sided tape centrally on the inside front cover of the plasma. Match the fold of the cream paper to the fold of the plasma and smooth the cream paper on to the front cover of the plasma.

 timing This card is quick and easy to mass-produce.

alternative White parchment, vellum and textured card would look good with silver angels and stars.

3 Cut out an 11 x 11.5cm (4¼ x 4½in) piece of cream parchment and use double-sided tape to attach it in a central position on the card front. Cut a piece of gold card, 9.5 x 10cm (3¾ x 4in), and tape it on the parchment. Finally, cut a piece of cream textured card, 9 x 9.5cm (3½ x 3¾in). Tape it on to the gold card.

coordinating items *Peel-offs usually come on a sheet containing a variety of designs, so use them to decorate other cards, gift-wrap, envelopes and gift pouches.*

4 Rule a thin, gold line around the edge of the parchment. Select your angel peel-off sticker and place it centrally on the card. Add a few gold stars to finish the design.

holly berries

Green textured handmade paper and a lovely holly sticker inspired this seasonal card.

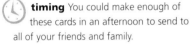

you will need

- A4 sheet green handmade paper
- Metal ruler
- Cutting mat
- Craft knife
- Pencil
- Stylus
- Small piece gold paper
- Double-sided tape
- Scissors
- Small piece gold paper
- Small piece red card
- Gold card
- Green angel hair paper
- Suitable holly sticker

timing You could make enough of these cards in an afternoon to send to all of your friends and family.

alternative Use this design as a starting point, but vary the colours – creams, golds and earthy colours would look good with a star sticker.

1 Cut a 21 x 12cm (8¼ x 4¾in) square from the handmade paper. Score and fold it to create the card blank.

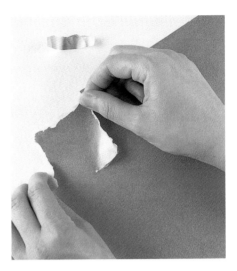

2 Tear out a 7.5cm (3in) square of gold paper. Tape it in a central position on the card so that it is a diamond shape.

3 Cut a 6cm (2½in) square of red card, attach it with double-sided tape centrally on the gold paper. Cut a 5.5cm (2¼in) square of gold card and tape it on top of the red card. Finally, cut a 5cm (2in) square of angel hair paper and place it on top of the gold card.

4 Place the holly sticker in a central position. To give your card a professional finish, place a sticker on the back of the card.

coordinating items *Use similar layered motifs to decorate gift pouches, boxes and tags. Make your own gift-wrap by stamping sprigs of holly on to tissue paper.*

winter wonderland

Stylized Christmas trees adorned with tiny silver jewels decorate this winter scene.

you will need

- A5 sheet silver card
- Craft knife
- Metal ruler
- Cutting mat
- Pencil
- Stylus
- Tracing paper or acetate
- A5 sheet green card
- Double-sided tape
- Scissors
- Tiny silver jewel stickers
- Red sequin stars
- PVA glue

timing Take time and care marking out the fold lines as precision is key when making a fold-out card.

alternative Use this idea to create your own designs; a row of sailing ships or pretty flowers would make effective cards.

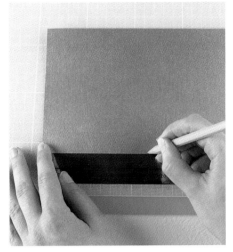

1 Cut a 21 x 13cm (8¼ x 5in) rectangle out of the silver card. On the card front make light pencil marks at 3.5cm (1½in), 10.5cm (4¼in) and 17.5cm (6⅞in). Score lines at these points. These lines will form the hill folds.

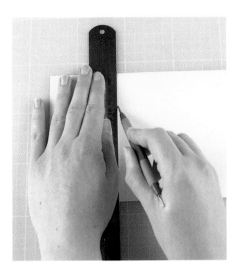

2 Turn the card over and mark points at 7cm (2¾in) and 14cm (5½in). Score lines at these points. These lines will form the valley folds. Fold along all of the lines you have scored to create the card base.

coordinating items Use the decorated trees to embellish gift-bags and tags. Wrap gifts in plain, coloured gift-wrap and stick on decorated trees.

3 Trace the tree templates on page 155. Use them to cut three large trees and four small trees out of green card. Referring to the photograph opposite, position the trees firmly in place using double-sided tape. Pay particular attention to how the trees overlap.

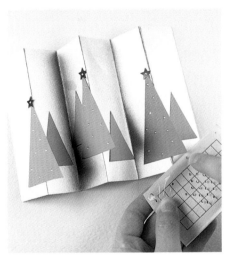

4 Decorate the trees with silver jewel stickers and star sequins. These jewels are tiny and extremely fiddly to use, so you may find sliding the jewel off the backing paper works better than lifting it.

star bright

Don't be afraid to use combinations of different materials on your cards. Foil,

handmade paper, corrugated card, textured paper and stickers work well together on

this sophisticated seasonal card.

you will need

- A5 sheet rich cream textured card
- Stylus
- Metal ruler
- Sheet gold foil
- Scissors
- Embossing board and star template
- Sheet natural handmade paper
- Sheet brown corrugated card
- Craft knife
- Cutting mat
- Double-sided tape
- Aerosol glue
- 3D tape
- Star peel-off stickers

timing This card simply involves layering, embossing and using stickers – all very easy.

alternative For a housewarming card emboss a simple house shape and decorate with tiny flower stickers or stamps.

1 Score and fold in half the sheet of textured card to create the card base. Cut a piece of gold foil 2.5cm (1in) square. Place it under the star template on the embossing board and use the stylus to emboss the shape. Take your time over this and work over the star image thoroughly so that it will have a good shape.

2 Prepare the layers. Cut a 7cm (2¾in) square of gold foil, tear two squares of handmade paper – one 6cm (2½in) and the other 3.5cm (1½in) and cut a 4.5cm (1¾in) square of corrugated card. Put double-sided tape on the undersides of the foil and corrugated card and spray the handmade paper squares with aerosol glue.

coordinating items
Make gift-bags using the same handmade paper you have used for the card and decorate with the star motif. Print plain gift-wrap with a complementary stamped and embossed snowflake design. You can also make alternative cards in other shapes and sizes and decorate them with the same star motif.

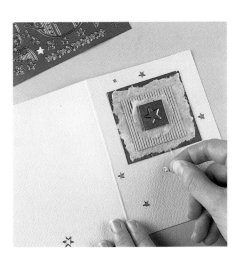

3 Place the larger piece of gold foil in a high central position on the card base. Next glue on the largest handmade paper square, followed by the corrugated card and finally the smaller torn paper square. Use 3D tape to attach the embossed star square in a central position. Decorate the card with star peel-off stickers.

robin redbreast

This robin redbreast will bring a little seasonal cheer to a Christmas mantlepiece.

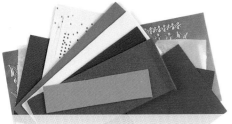

you will need

- A5 sheet blue ribbed card
- Craft knife
- Metal ruler
- Cutting mat
- Pencil
- Stylus
- Tracing paper/ acetate

- Blue, white, red, brown and orange foam sheets
- Scissors
- Sheet red card
- Double-sided tape
- Tiny jewel stickers
- Gold star stickers

1 Measure and cut out a 21 x 10.5cm (8¼ x 4in) rectangle of blue ribbed card. Score and fold to create the base.

2 Trace the templates on page 155.

3 Use the templates to cut out the foam shapes for the robin and the background. When cutting the background cut out an 8.5cm (3½in) square from the blue and white foam sheets. Lay one on top of the other and place the background template on top. Cut through all three layers.

4 Cut a 9cm (3¾in) square of red card. Use double-sided tape to attach the sky and snow background to it. Next attach the body, legs and hat. Cut the beak from a scrap of orange foam and tape in place.

5 Stick on the tiny jewel eyes and place the gold star stickers on the blue sky background.

🕐 **timing** This card takes a little time to make so choose a few special friends to send it to.

📦 **alternative** Create a country scene with green fields, blue sky and a white sheep. You could add some fluffy clouds too.

coordinating items
Use scraps of foam to create your own designs and use them to decorate cards, tags and boxes.

festive garland

This card is simple and sophisticated. The clean white card sets off the

bright green holly garland and is highlighted by the brilliant red berries.

you will need

- A5 sheet white textured card
- Pencil
- Metal ruler
- Craft knife
- Cutting mat
- Stylus
- Holly leaf punch
- Green paper
- Pair of compasses
- PVA glue
- 3D red paint
- Red ribbon bow

timing Attaching the holly sprigs can be time consuming.

alternative Make this card in silver and hot pink to create an entirely different mood, or set the holly garland against a rich red background to put a little warmth on to a friend's mantlepiece. You might use a sticker or mini Christmas decoration instead of a bow as a feature.

1 Cut a 17 x 14cm (6¾ x 5½in) rectangle from the white textured card. Score and fold in half to create the card base. Punch about 40 holly sprigs from green paper.

2 Lightly draw a 5cm (2in) circle in an upper central position on the card. Squeeze dots of PVA glue around the circle. Lay the holly sprigs around the circle, working in one direction, but lean the sprigs to the right and left to create a thick garland.

3 Once the glue is dry, squeeze dots of red 3D paint in groups of two or three around the garland.

4 Attach the ribbon bow with PVA glue. For a professional finish you may want to glue a holly sprig on the back of the card and use it to decorate an envelope.

christmas pudding

The motif on this card was created using an embossed stamped design. Use up lots of those odd-sized pieces of paper and card in your workbox to create other motifs.

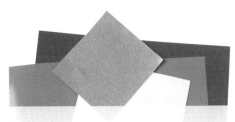

you will need

- A5 sheet red card
- Stylus
- Metal ruler
- Embossing pad
- Christmas pudding rubber stamp
- White card
- Scrap paper
- Bronze embossing powder
- Tweezers or tongs
- Precision heat tool
- Felt-tip pens
- Craft knife
- Cutting mat
- Pencil
- Scissors
- Double-sided tape
- Red paper
- Green paper
- Gold paper

timing Spend a few hours making lots of different motifs. This design is ideal for seasonal mass-production.

alternative Use stickers, stamps, peel-offs and punches to create seasonal motifs.

1   Score and fold the sheet of red card to create the card base. Set aside. Using the embossing pad, print a Christmas pudding on to white card. Fold a sheet of scrap paper in half and open it out. Put the stamped white card on to the scrap paper and sprinkle it with bronze embossing powder. Shake the excess powder on to the scrap paper and return it to the container. Holding the card with tweezers or tongs, seal the design with the precision heat tool.

2   Colour in the pudding, leaves and berries using felt-tip pens. Measure a square around the image leaving a 0.5cm (¼in) border. Cut out.

3   Use double-sided tape to attach the image to red paper. Cut away all but a narrow border. Layer on to green paper and cut a narrow border, and then gold paper and cut a narrow border. Tape the layered image on to white card and cut away all but a 0.5cm (¼in) border.

4   Fold a sheet of scrap paper in half and open it out. Sprinkle some bronze embossing powder on to the paper. Press the edges of the motif into the embossing pad and then into the embossing powder. Holding the motif with tweezers or tongs, seal with the precision heat tool. Attach the complete motif in an upper central position on the card.

gallery
daisy punch

Stylish, simple and quick to put together, these cards all have a crisp, clean look and were created using the same daisy punch. Punches are easy to use with paper or thin card. I particularly enjoyed using thin card because once the daisies were stuck in place I was able to raise the petals slightly to create a three-dimensional effect. All of the cards have been embellished with 3D paint.

1 A white card base provides a stylish background for three red daisies. Punch out the daisies and attach them to a square of card. Cut simple stalks and leaves and use PVA glue to stick in place. Layer them up over coordinating colours and tape the motif in an upper central position. Embellish with yellow 3D paint.

2 This card is tall and slim, in fact it would make a good bookmark! Attach the daisies in a random fashion and choose subtle colours for the layers to focus attention on the daisies. Use red and yellow 3D paint to decorate.

3 Using corrugated card gives this design an entirely different look. Stamp and emboss a vase design on thin card. Cut it out and stick on the card. The horizontal stripes give the impression of a tablecloth.

4 This card can be displayed horizontally or vertically. The design is simple – white daisies with yellow centres on a blue card base.

5 Another stamped vase graces this card; embellish the pastel shades with silver 3D paint. Using pale colours gives this card an entirely different look.

6 Three daisies in a row. There is something about threes – two is too few, four is too many! This design would look good in almost any colour scheme.

7 Once again a simple design – three daisy motifs, layered and decorated with 3D paint. Use a punch to make the holes for the ribbon. You might want to add an insert on which to write a greeting.

1

2

3

4

6

5

7

gallery

indigo blue paper

The wonderful blue of this striking gift-wrap reminded me of Africa, Indonesia and many other cultures with histories rich in art and design. A sheet of gift-wrap can inspire many different card designs.

1 A gift-bag is quick and easy to make (see page 21). Tie it with an organza bow and decorate with a special photograph layered on to blue card.

2 This little gift-tag is simplicity itself. Card layers decorated with a craft wire heart.

3 Emboss a simple design on to copper foil. Attach the foil feature to a gift-wrap background and frame with thin ribbons of the same paper.

4 A gift-tag simply decorated with a single punched flower. Make a hole with a punch and attach a gold tie.

5 Wrap a box in the gift-wrapping and tie with gold cord.

6 Make a dark blue card base and create a motif made up of three layers – white card, gift-wrap, white card. Punch the flowers out of finely corrugated card and attach with 3D tape. Draw the stems with green 3D paint.

7 I used the paper design to my advantage on this card. Form a grid of white paper ribbons and draw a flower with white 3D paint.

8 Blue handmade paper and yellow card give this greetings card a very different feel. Embellish the gift-wrap with yellow 3D paint.

1

2

3

4

5

6

7

8

gallery

peacock feather stamp

This stamp is stylish, simple and inspirational. Purchasing a stamp can stretch your budget, but they are so versatile, as this gallery shows.

1 Emboss a pink feather on vellum and edge with green glitter. Attach the design to a red handmade paper base.

2 Use yellow card as a base. Cut a frame of yellow angel hair paper, with a deeper edge at the bottom. Stamp the feather on to the card and emboss in gold. Decorate with gold glitter.

3 Stamp the feather on to black card and emboss in baby pink. Edge the tag with baby pink embossing powder. Punch a hole in the end and thread with pink ribbon.

4 Stamp the feather on to vellum and emboss in red glitter. Cut out the design and back with white card. Layer on to vellum and red card. Attach the motif to a white card base.

5 Colour the stamp with blue, purple and green felt-tip pens. Stamp on to a piece of patterned white paper. Cut in to a diamond shape and back with silver card.

6 Stamp the image on to vellum and cut out. Attach to white, textured card. Leaving a fairly wide border, trim with deckle-edged scissors. Tape the motif slightly to the right of a pink card base. Punch two holes at the left edge, thread pink ribbon and tie a bow.

7 Decorate a white gift pouch. Use a scrap of paper to cover the part of the stamp that you do not want on the printed image.

8 Colour the stamp with purple, green and blue felt-tips pens. Back the stamped image in white card and layer up on gold, purple and dark blue card. Attach the motif to a white card base with 3D tape.

9 Colour the stamp with felt-tip pens as before and stamp on to vellum. Back with a small rectangle of white card. Use a border of gold paper ribbons and silver 3D paint to highlight.

5

8

6

7

9

gallery

paper rosebuds

Red roses signify romance, while pink roses carry loving thoughts. White roses lend themselves to serenity, making them more suited to cards with deep, emotional messages. Rosebuds can be tied to simply wrapped gifts (you might want to use freshly-picked rosebuds to carry a special romantic message). To create coordinating gift-wrap, stamp roses on to tissue paper, stencil them on to coloured paper and embossed buds on to brown paper.

1 A simply wrapped gift: red tissue paper decorated with red rosebuds and tied with green ribbon.

2 A white card base with a layered feature. Attach the rosebuds to a rectangle of white card covered with green angel hair paper. Tie with a bow sticker. Surround the design with gold 3D paint dots.

3 Wrap a bunch of paper roses in tissue paper and attach to subtly coloured card layers.

4 Hearts and flowers – what more could a loved one ask for? Cut a heart-shaped frame out of red card. Attach the flowers and tie with a silver bow. Finish off the design with dots of red 3D paint.

5 Photocopy a suitable photograh on to acetate. Cut out a section and layer it on to white card. Attach the bunch of roses and tie with a ribbon of red card.

4

3

5

gallery

stickers and motifs

Stickers, peel-offs and cut-outs are used here to good effect. The range of stickers available is almost endless, so you can decorate a gift for any occasion and personalize it for the recipient. Peel-offs and stickers are best attached once the gift is wrapped, then you can place them where they will not be covered by the ribbon.

1 and **2** You will need suitable champagne bottle and glass party sequins. Attach them to violet tissue paper using PVA glue. Scatter tiny dots of glue on the paper, bearing in mind the pattern that you want to create with the sequins. Use pretty ribbon to finish off the parcel.

3 This gift-wrap is so quick and easy to make. Simply decorate a sheet of deep blue tissue paper with peel-off gold stars.

4 These red cracker, gold streamer and star stickers on white tissue paper create a sophisticated look. Tie the gift with green starry ribbon for a seasonal feel.

5 I cut these pumpkins from a Hallowe'en streamer. The orange pumpkins look great on the green background and the tiny star stickers add a little magic to the paper. Use PVA glue to attach the motifs.

6 These ghosts were cut from a Hallowe'en streamer too. Use PVA glue to attach the images. Decorate a gift wrapped in this paper with an orange ribbon bow.

7 Decorate a brown paper bag with a layered motif. Cut a square of green tissue paper and attach it using aerosol glue to a square of gold card. Layer this onto green and then orange card. Decorate with pumpkins and gold star stickers.

gallery
rubber stamps

Card-makers are now spoilt for choice when it comes to rubber stamps. If you decorate a card with a stamp you might want to use the same stamp to decorate tissue paper or a gift-bag, box or pouch. Making a set of coordinating items couldn't be simpler. If you want to be a little more adventurous, emboss the stamped design using embossing powders and seal using a precision heat tool (see page 14).

1 Stamp Christmas puddings in gold onto bright red tissue paper. Emboss with gold embossing powder and seal with a precision heat tool. The stamped design would also look good if stamped and embossed in a bright red or green on brown paper.

2 I haven't actually used a rubber stamp here! Simply use dots of 3D paint running in a freehand design to create a decorative pattern. You could use a simple rubber stamp to create a similar effect.

3 Stamp bright yellow tissue paper with a Christmas candle design. Emboss the designs with bronze embossing powder and seal with a precision heat tool. Colour with felt-tip pens. Use a plain layer of tissue beneath the decorated layer so that the present inside is completely concealed.

4 and **5** White daisies on a sky blue background give a fresh country feel. Stamp the daisy in white, sprinkle with white embossing powder and seal with a precision heat tool. Draw the leaves using an embossing pen, sprinkle with green embossing powder and seal. Put a dot of yellow 3D paint in the centre of each daisy. Finish the parcel off with a blue and white gingham ribbon bow.

6 and **7** A very different look created with the same daisy stamp as used on items 4 and 5. Hot pink tissue paper printed with white daisies – great for a fashionable friend's birthday gift. Use a gauze ribbon to tie up the parcel.

3

6

4

5

7

gallery
stencils

Create your own stencil by drawing a simple shape onto card and cut it out using a craft knife. An even simpler way is to use a punch to cut a shape from the card. You can use a dauber pen, stamp pad, embossing powders (sealed using a precision heat tool; see page 14) or paint to colour the design.

1 A sophisticated design in black and white. Use a flower punch to create the stencil. Print the design using a clear stamp pad, sprinkle with white embossing powder and seal using a precision heat tool. Put a dot of 3D paint in the centre of each flower.

2 The same stencil as used on item 1 has been used here to create quite a different effect. Stencil the summery yellow tissue paper using a purple stamp pad. Use clear embossing powder to give the flowers a special finish. Seal using a precision heat tool. Put a dot of yellow 3D paint in the centre of each flower.

3 This wrapping paper has been decorated using the same stencil as used on items 1 and 2. This time stencil and emboss red flowers onto white tissue paper.

4 and **5** Create a star stencil by drawing a star onto thin card and cutting it out with a craft knife or use a star punch. Stamp the star shape onto the blue tissue paper using a clear stamp pad and then emboss using silver embossing powder. Seal using a precision heat tool.

6 Stencil hot pink tissue paper in exactly the same way as described for items 4 and 5. A silver ribbon would look good with this paper.

7 Multi-coloured stars created with the same star stencil as used for items 4, 5 and 6 brighten up a sheet of yellow tissue paper. Stencil the stars in different colours and use clear embossing powder to give them a shiny finish.

8 Follow the instructions for item 5, but use gold embossing powder instead. Red tissue stencilled in gold creates a wonderful Christmassy feel.

9 Buy a plain, coloured gift-bag and decorate it with stencilled stars. If you are unable to buy a bag in the colour that you want, simply make one following the instructions on page 21.

gallery

handmade paper

There are so many beautiful handmade papers available to tempt the card-maker. Plain, coloured or textured paper provides a good base for stamping or stencilling and narrow bands of paper containing leaves, flowers and other decorative features are wonderful for embellishing gifts.

1 Take turquoise handmade paper as a base. Use an embossing pen to mark some very simple branch shapes. Emboss with brown embossing powder and seal with a precision heat tool (see page 14). Punch out small pink flower shapes. Use PVA glue to attach the flowers to the branches in groups of two or three and scatter a few randomly between the branches. Paint a spot of pink 3D paint in the centre of each flower and dot green 3D paint around the flowers to represent leaves. Finally, tie a green ribbon around the parcel.

2 Stamp daisies onto white tissue paper using a clear stamp pad and then emboss them with pink embossing powder. Seal with a precision heat tool (see page 14). Use a leaf stamp or draw leaves freehand with an embossing pen. Emboss with green embossing powder and seal.

3 Wrap a gift in red handmade paper and place a band of white decorative paper around it. Finish with a small bunch of paper rosebuds attached using PVA glue. This would be perfect wrapping for a Valentine's gift.

4 Make a small gift-bag from pumpkin-yellow handmade paper (follow the instructions for making gift-bags on page 21). Punch holes through the top of the bag and thread with a fine cord tie. Decorate the bag with a sprig of paper bamboo leaves.

5 Wrap a gift in pink silver-threaded handmade paper and decorate with a band of white textured paper. Embellish with pink ribbon and a sprig of paper leaves and flowers.

6 This parcel has a simple country feel. Wrap a gift in green handmade paper then attach a length of gingham ribbon around the centre of the gift. Cut heart shapes out of red handmade paper and stick onto the ribbon.

templates

The templates shown here are actual size
unless otherwise stated. They may be easily
enlarged or reduced on a photocopier if you
wish to make a larger or smaller card.

How does your garden grow?
(page 30)

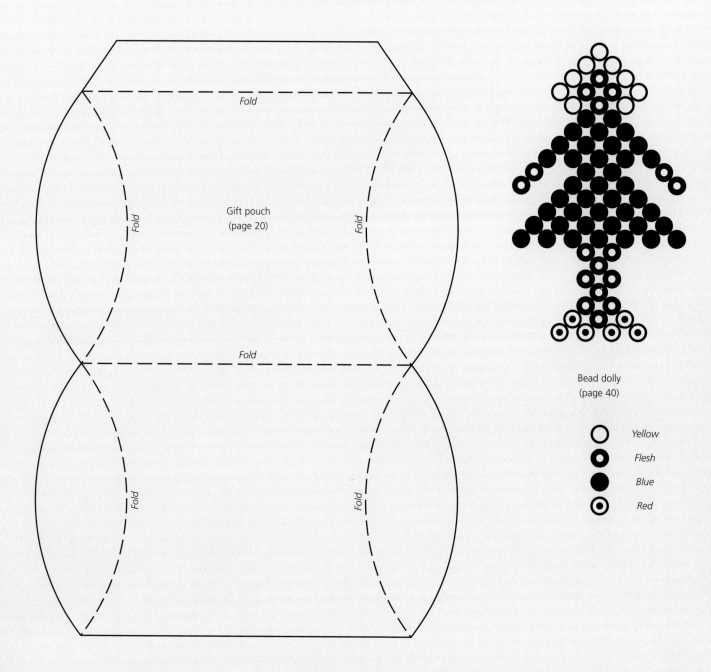

Gift pouch
(page 20)

Fold

Fold

Fold

Fold

Fold

Fold

Bead dolly
(page 40)

○ *Yellow*

◉ *Flesh*

● *Blue*

◎ *Red*

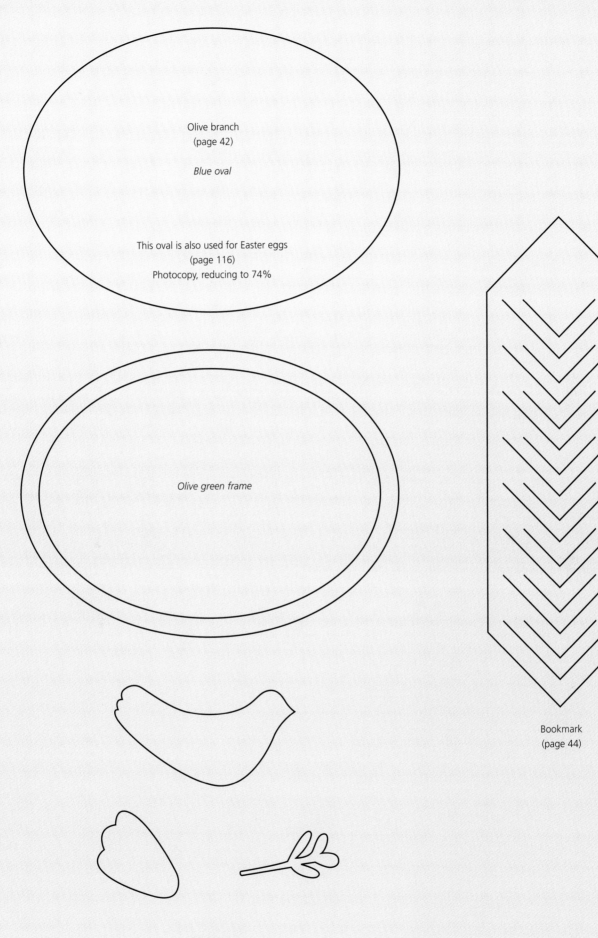

Olive branch
(page 42)

Blue oval

This oval is also used for Easter eggs
(page 116)
Photocopy, reducing to 74%

Olive green frame

Bookmark
(page 44)

Olive branch
(page 42)

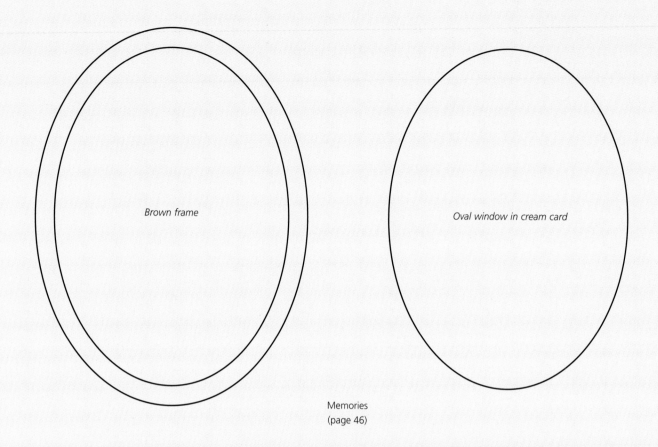

Brown frame

Oval window in cream card

Memories
(page 46)

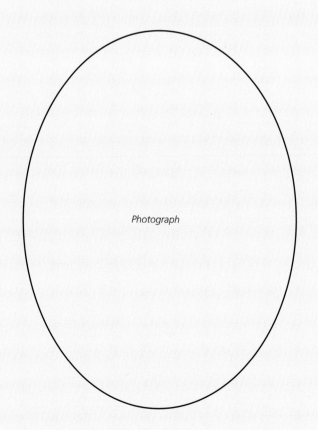

Photograph

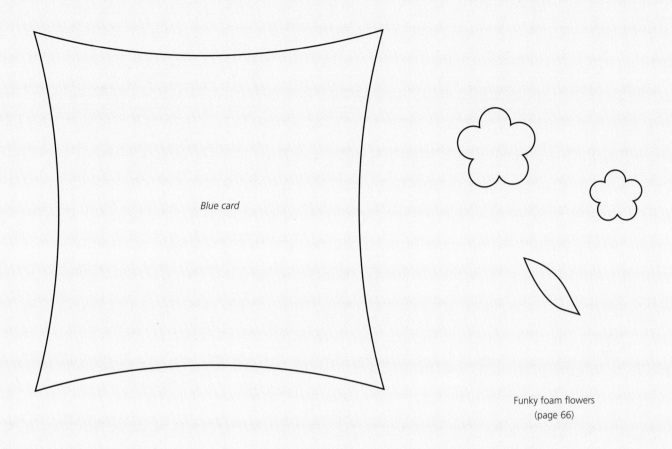

Blue card

Funky foam flowers
(page 66)

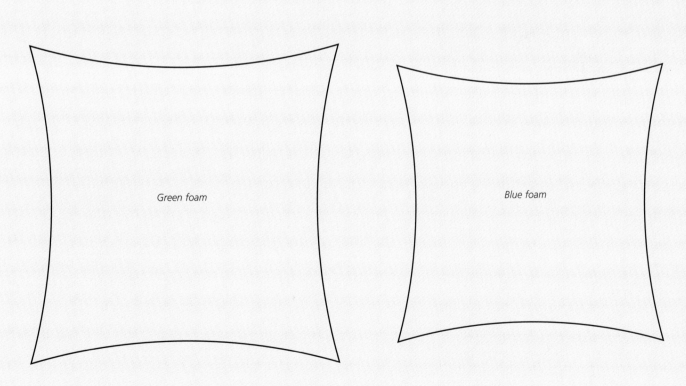

Green foam

Blue foam

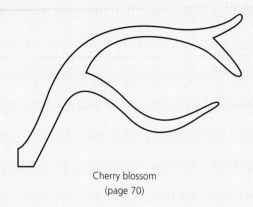

Cherry blossom
(page 70)

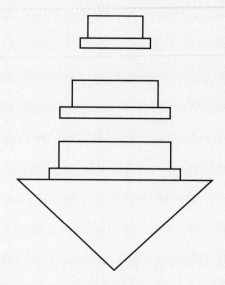

Wedding cake
(page 90)

Patchwork house
(page 80)

Tiny togs
(page 94)

Sparkling hearts
(page 86)

Happy hallowe'en
(page 104)

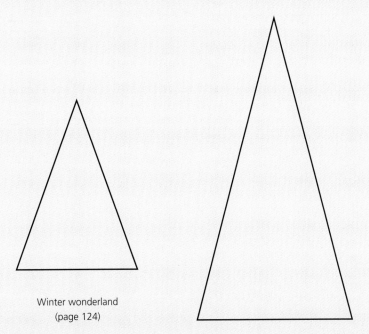

Winter wonderland
(page 124)

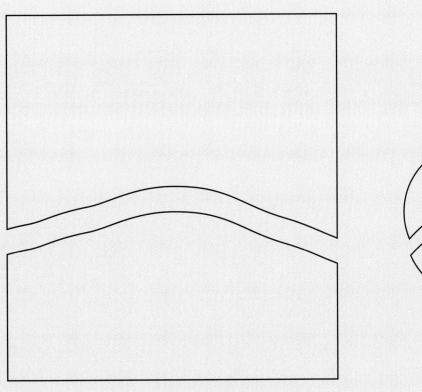

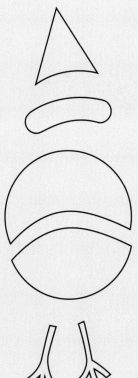

Robin redbreast
(page 128)

Magic number
(page 106)

suppliers list

United Kingdom

L. Cornelissen & Son Ltd
105 Great Russell Street
London WC1B 3RY
Tel: 020 7636 1045
Also:
1A Hercules Street
London N7 6AT
Tel: 020 7281 8870
General craft supplier.

Cowling & Wilcox
26-28 Broadwick Street
London W1F 8HX
Tel: 020 7734 9557
www.cowlingandwilcox.com
Email: art@cowlingandwilcox.com
General craft supplier.

Craft Creations
Ingersoll House
Delamare Road
Cheshunt
Hertfordshire EN8 9ND
Tel: 01992 781 900
www.craftcreations.com
Email: enquiries@craftcreations.com
General craft supplier.

Cranberry Card Company
Unit 4 Greenway Workshops
Bedwas House Ind. Est.
Bedwas
Caephilly CF83 8DW
Tel 02920 807941
www.cranberrycards.co.uk
Email: info@cranberrycards.co.uk
Selection of card, paper and accessories.

The English Stamp Company
Worth Matravers
Dorset BH19 3JP
Tel: 01929 439 117
www.englishstamp.com
Email: sales@englishstamp.com
Suppliers of stamps, paints, inkpads and handmade paper. Mail-order only.

Falkiner Fine Papers Ltd
76 Southampton Row
London WC1B 4AR
Tel: 020 7831 1151
Carries a large range of handmade papers. Also offers a mail-order service.

Homecrafts Direct
Unit 2, Wanlip Rd Syston
Leicester
Leicestershire LE7 1PD
Tel: 0116 269 7733
www.homecrafts.co.uk
Email: info@homecrafts.co.uk
Mail-order service. Selection of handmade papers and range of craft products.

Lakeland Limited
Alexandra Buildings
Windermere
Cumbria LA23 1BQ
Tel: 015394 88100
www.lakelandlimited.com
Email: net.shop@lakelandlimited.co.uk
Range of craft products available. Mail-order service and stores nationwide.

T N Lawrence
208 Portland Rd
Hove, East Sussex
BN3 5QT
Tel: 01273 260260
www.lawrence.co.uk
Carries a large range of papers as well as general artist's materials.

Paperchase
Flagship Store and Main Office
213 Tottenham Court Road
London W1T 7PS
Tel: 020 7467 6200
Retailers of stationery, wrapping paper and art materials. Call for your nearest outlet.
Mail order service
Tel: 0161 839 1500
www.paperchase.co.uk
Email: mailorder@paperchase.co.uk

Sew Simple
Unit 16 Taverham Garden Centre
Covert Road
Taverham NR8 6HT
Tel: 01603 262 870
www.sew-simple.co.uk

The Stencil Store
41A Heronsgate Road
Chorleywood
Herts WD3 5BL
Tel: 01923 285577
www.stencilstore.com
Email: stencilstore@onetel.com
Supply wide range of stencil designs. Phone for nearest store or to order catalogue.

Australia

Artwise Amazing Paper
186 Enmore Road
Enmore, NSW 2042
Tel: 02 9519 8237
www.amazingpaper.com.au

Lincraft
www.lincraft.com.au
General craft supplier.
Stores throughout Australia

Myer Centre, Rundle Mall
Adelaide, SA 5000
Tel: 02 8231 6611

Myer Centre, Queen Street
Brisbane, QLD 4000
Tel: 07 3221 0064

Shop D02/D03
Canberra Centre, Bunda Street
Canberra, ACT 2601
Tel: 02 6257 4516

Australia on Collins
Melbourne, VIC 3000
Tel: 03 9650 1609

Imperial Arcade, Pitt Street
Sydney, NSW 2000
Tel: 02 9221 5111

Paper Fantasy
256a Charters Towers Road
Hermit Park, QLD 4812
Tel: 07 4725 1272

Paperwright
124 Lygon Street
Carlton, VIC 3053
Tel: 03 9663 8747

Spotlight
Tel: 1800 656 256
www.spotlight.com.au
General craft supplier.
Call for nearest store.

South Africa

Art Shop
140A Victoria Avenue
Benoni West
1503
Tel / Fax: 011 421 1030

Arts, Crafts and Hobbies
72 Hibernia Street
George 6529
Tel / Fax: 044 874 1337
Mail-order service available.

Pen and Art
Shop 313, Musgrave Centre
Musgrave Road
Durban 4001
Tel / Fax: 031 201 0094

Bowker Arts and Crafts
52 4th Avenue
Newton Park
Port Elizabeth 6001
Tel: 041 365 2487
Fax: 041 365 5306

Centurion Kuns
Shop 45, Eldoraigne Shopping Mall
Saxby Road
Eldoraigne 0157
Tel / Fax: 012 654 0449

Crafty Supplies
Shop UG 2, Stadium on Main
Main Road, Claremont 7700
Cape Town
Tel: 021 671 0286
Fax: 021 671 0308

Creative Papercraft
64 Judd Street
Horizon 1724
Tel / Fax: 011 763 5682

L & P Stationery and Art
141 Zastron Street
Westdene
Bloemfontein 9301
Tel: 051 430 1085
Fax: 051 430 4102

Le Papier du Port
Gardens Centre
Cape Town 8000
Tel: 021 462 4796
Fax: 021 461 9281
Mail-order service available.

Scarab Paper
Next to Engen Garage on the N2 between
Sedgefield and George
Tel: 044 343 2455
Fax: 044 343 1828
Email: scarabpaper@mweb.co.za

New Zealand

Brush & Palette
50 Lichfield Street
Christchurch
Tel / Fax: 03 366 3088

Fine Art Papers
200 Madras Street
Christchurch
Tel: 03 379 4410
Fax: 03 379 4443

Gordon Harris Art Supplies
4 Gillies Ave
Newmarket
Auckland
Tel: 09 520 4466
Fax: 09 520 0880
and
31 Symonds St
Auckland Central
Tel: 09 377 9992

Littlejohns
170 Victoria Street
Wellington
Tel: 04 385 2099
Fax: 04 385 2090

Studio Art Supplies
81 Parnell Rise
Parnell
Auckland
Tel: 09 377 0302
Fax: 09 377 7657

G Webster & Co Ltd
44 Manners Street
Wellington
Tel: 04 384 2134
Fax: 04 384 2968

index